First World War
and Army of Occupation
War Diary
France, Belgium and Germany

18 DIVISION
Divisional Troops
Divisional Ammunition Column
26 June 1915 - 31 March 1919

WO95/2026/2

The Naval & Military Press Ltd
www.nmarchive.com
Published in association with The National Archives

Published by

The Naval & Military Press Ltd

Unit 10 Ridgewood Industrial Park,

Uckfield, East Sussex,

TN22 5QE England

Tel: +44 (0) 1825 749494

www.naval-military-press.com

www.nmarchive.com

This diary has been reprinted in facsimile from the original. Any imperfections are inevitably reproduced and the quality may fall short of modern type and cartographic standards.

© **Crown Copyright**
Images reproduced by permission of The National Archives, London, England, 2015.

Contents

Document type	Place/Title	Date From	Date To
Heading	WO95/2026-2		
Heading	18th Division 18th Divl Ammn Col. Aug 1915-Mar 1919		
War Diary	Heytesbury	26/06/1915	27/06/1915
War Diary	Warminster	27/06/1915	27/06/1915
War Diary	South-Hampton	27/06/1915	27/06/1915
War Diary	Le Havre	28/06/1915	28/06/1915
War Diary	Monton-Villers	29/06/1915	29/06/1915
Heading	18th Division 18th Divl. Q.C. Vol. I Aug Sept 15		
War Diary	Montonvillers	01/08/1915	08/08/1915
War Diary	Beaucourt	11/08/1915	27/08/1915
War Diary	Bonnay	02/09/1915	30/09/1915
Heading	18th Division 18th D.A.C. Vol 2 Vol 2 Oct 15		
War Diary	Bonnay	01/10/1915	31/10/1915
Heading	18th Division 18th D.A.C. Vol 3 Nov 15		
War Diary	Bonnay	11/11/1915	29/11/1915
War Diary	Bonnay	01/11/1915	09/11/1915
Heading	18th Division 18th D.A.C. Vol. 4 Dec 15		
War Diary	Bonnay	01/12/1915	31/12/1915
Heading	85th Bde. A.C. Vol. 6 Jan 16		
War Diary	Treux	01/01/1916	31/01/1916
Heading	18th D.A.C Vol 5		
War Diary	Bonnay	01/01/1916	08/01/1916
War Diary	Bonnay	03/01/1916	30/01/1916
Heading	85th Bde Amm Column Vol VII		
Miscellaneous	From O.C. 85th Bde. Amn Column R.F.A.		
War Diary	Treux	01/02/1916	01/02/1916
War Diary	Lavie'ville	06/02/1916	29/02/1916
Heading	18th Div Amm Col Vol. 6		
War Diary	Bonnay	02/02/1916	05/02/1916
War Diary	Pont Noyelle	06/02/1916	27/02/1916
War Diary	Bonnay	02/02/1916	05/02/1916
War Diary	Pont Noyelle	06/02/1916	27/02/1916
Heading	18 Div A.Col Vol 7		
War Diary	Pont Noyelle	01/03/1916	05/03/1916
War Diary	Bussy Les Dours	06/03/1916	21/03/1916
War Diary	Chipilly	23/03/1916	30/03/1916
Heading	85 Bde Amm C. Vol 8		
War Diary	Lavie'ville	01/03/1916	01/03/1916
War Diary	Bussy Les Daours	03/03/1916	03/03/1916
War Diary	Bois Des Tailles	09/03/1916	31/03/1916
War Diary	Chipilly	01/04/1916	28/04/1916
War Diary	Bois Gressaire	01/04/1916	30/04/1916
War Diary	Chipilly	03/05/1916	06/05/1916
War Diary	Argoeuves	07/05/1916	28/05/1916
Heading	From O.C 8.5th Bde Ammtn Col		
War Diary	Bois Gressaire	01/05/1916	17/05/1916
War Diary	Argoeuves	01/06/1916	10/06/1916
War Diary	Grovetown Camp	11/06/1916	23/06/1916
War Diary	Bois Des Tailles	24/06/1916	30/06/1916

Heading	18th Divn. Ammunition Column		
War Diary	K. 18. Central (France 62 d)	01/07/1916	16/07/1916
War Diary	F. 19.b 8.9 (France 62d)	17/07/1916	20/07/1916
War Diary	F. 19.b 8.9. (62d France) Argoeuves	21/07/1916	27/07/1916
War Diary	Eecke	28/07/1916	01/08/1916
War Diary	Le Kirlem (Hazebrouk 5a-Map)	03/08/1916	06/08/1916
War Diary	Le Kirlem	06/08/1916	19/08/1916
War Diary	Le Kirlem (Near Steenwerk)	20/08/1916	22/08/1916
War Diary	Le Kirlem	22/08/1916	28/08/1916
War Diary	Authuile	29/08/1916	29/08/1916
War Diary	Val De Maison	30/08/1916	31/08/1916
Miscellaneous	Memorandum On Appendix I		
Miscellaneous	Channels of Ammunition Supply (Outwards) From 18th Divisional Amm. Col. Appendix II.	12/08/1916	12/08/1916
Miscellaneous	The Following Will Be The Location of Units of 18th Division In The New Area, Reference Map Sheets 36 B And 51 C 1/140,000.	20/08/1916	20/08/1916
Heading	War Diary 18th D.A.C.		
War Diary	Val De Maison	01/09/1916	02/09/1916
War Diary	Albert	03/09/1916	19/09/1916
War Diary	Albert Area.	20/09/1916	30/09/1916
Operation(al) Order(s)	18th Divisional Artillery Order No. 9 by Brig. General S.F. Metcalfe, D.S.O. App I.	02/09/1916	02/09/1916
Miscellaneous	Amendments to 18th Divisional Artillery Operation Order No. 9.	02/09/1916	02/09/1916
Miscellaneous	18th. Divisional Artillery. No. 10. By Brig. Gen. S.F. Metcalfe, D.S.O. App II		
Miscellaneous	Subject. Clearing the Battlefield. App. III	14/09/1916	14/09/1916
Miscellaneous	18th Div. No. Q.R. 6 App IV.	15/09/1916	15/09/1916
Miscellaneous	O.C. 18th. D.A.C. App. V	17/09/1916	17/09/1916
Heading	War Diary For October 1916 18th Div. Amm. Col Vol 14		
War Diary	Albert	01/10/1916	31/10/1916
Heading	War Diary For November 1916 18th D.A.C. Vol 15		
War Diary	Albert	01/11/1916	30/11/1916
Heading	War Diary of 18th Divisional Ammunition Column R.F.A. From December 1st 1916. To December 31st 1916 (Volume VI)		
War Diary	Albert	01/12/1916	05/12/1916
War Diary	L'Heure	06/12/1916	01/01/1917
War Diary	Geuschart.	02/01/1917	02/01/1917
War Diary	Mezorelles	03/01/1917	03/01/1917
War Diary	Marieux	04/01/1917	04/01/1917
War Diary	Senlis.	05/01/1917	23/01/1917
War Diary	Near Senlis	24/01/1917	31/01/1917
Heading	18th D.A.C. Vol 18		
War Diary	Senlis	01/02/1917	28/02/1917
Heading	War Diary For March 1917. 18th Divisional Ammunition Column. Vol 19		
Miscellaneous	Officer To R Q & R A Records Headquarters 18th Div Arty	06/05/1917	06/05/1917
Heading	War Diary For April. 1917 18th D.A.C. Vol 20		
War Diary	Authville	01/04/1917	25/04/1917
War Diary	Rubempre	26/04/1917	26/04/1917
War Diary	Beauval	27/04/1917	27/04/1917
War Diary	Beauvoir	28/04/1917	28/04/1917

War Diary	Riviere	28/04/1917	28/04/1917
War Diary	Aubrometz	29/04/1917	29/04/1917
War Diary	Bergueneuse	30/04/1917	30/04/1917
War Diary	Fontes.	31/04/1917	31/04/1917
War Diary	Hazebrouck	01/04/1917	23/04/1917
War Diary	Oblinghem	24/04/1917	30/04/1917
Heading	War Diary For May. 1917. 18th D.A.C. Vol 21		
War Diary	Boisleux St. Marc.	01/05/1917	14/05/1917
War Diary	Boiry St Martin	15/05/1917	30/05/1917
Heading	18th D.A.C. June 1917 Vol 22		
War Diary	Boiry St Martin	01/06/1917	30/06/1917
Miscellaneous	Officer To R.H. & R.C. Records H45 Headquarters 1st Div Artillery Herewith War Diary For July 1917.		
War Diary	Boiry St Martin	03/07/1917	10/07/1917
War Diary	Eecke	11/07/1917	11/07/1917
War Diary	H26a & b	12/07/1917	14/07/1917
War Diary	H.26 a	14/07/1917	24/07/1917
War Diary	H32c	25/07/1917	31/07/1917
War Diary	H 32c W of Dickebusch	01/08/1917	03/08/1917
War Diary	H c 32	03/08/1917	26/08/1917
War Diary	H c 32	02/08/1917	06/08/1917
War Diary	H 32 c	10/08/1917	28/08/1917
War Diary	H 32 c	08/08/1917	08/08/1917
War Diary	H 32 c	04/08/1917	08/08/1917
War Diary	H 32 c	07/08/1917	23/08/1917
War Diary	Oudezeele.	01/09/1917	19/09/1917
War Diary	Serques.	20/09/1917	24/09/1917
War Diary	Eringhem	25/09/1917	25/09/1917
War Diary	Peselhoek	27/09/1917	27/09/1917
War Diary	H.2 A. 6.4. A 28.d. 3.6. A 22 a.1.7. (Sheet 28 NW)	29/09/1917	29/09/1917
War Diary	Camp Near Vlamertinghe	30/09/1917	30/09/1917
Heading	18th Div. Ammn. Column. War Diary For Month of October, 1917		
War Diary	Dac. Wagon Lines Near Vlamertinghe	01/10/1917	13/10/1917
War Diary	Wagon Lines Nr. Vlamertinghe.	13/10/1917	26/10/1917
War Diary	Wagon Lines Near Vlamertinghe.	27/10/1917	31/10/1917
War Diary	Wagon Lines Near Vlamertinghe	01/10/1917	31/10/1917
War Diary	H.2.a.6.4 Vlamertinghe.	01/11/1917	30/11/1917
War Diary	H.2.a.6.4 Vlamertinghe. (Sheet. 28.N.W.)	01/11/1917	30/11/1917
War Diary	Wagon Lines Near Vlamertinghe	01/12/1917	12/12/1917
War Diary	Crombeke	13/12/1917	01/01/1918
War Diary	Wagon Lines. Near Boesinghe	01/01/1918	30/01/1918
War Diary	Wagon Lines Near Boesinghe.	01/01/1918	30/01/1918
War Diary	Wagon Lines Near Hamhoek	30/01/1918	31/01/1918
War Diary	Hamhoek.	01/01/1918	10/01/1918
War Diary	Pont L'Eveqe	11/01/1918	15/01/1918
War Diary	Guiscard	15/01/1918	27/01/1918
War Diary	Rouez	28/01/1918	28/01/1918
War Diary	Hamhoek	01/01/1918	10/01/1918
War Diary	Pont L'Eveqe	11/01/1918	15/01/1918
War Diary	Guiscard	15/01/1918	27/01/1918
War Diary	Rouez	28/01/1918	28/01/1918
War Diary	Hamhoek.	01/02/1918	10/02/1918
War Diary	Pont L'Eveqe.	11/02/1918	15/02/1918
War Diary	Guiscard	15/02/1918	27/02/1918
War Diary	Rouez	28/02/1918	28/02/1918

War Diary	Hamhoek	01/02/1918	10/02/1918
War Diary	Pont L'Eveqe	11/02/1918	15/02/1918
War Diary	Guiscard	15/02/1918	27/02/1918
War Diary	Rouez.	28/02/1918	28/02/1918
Heading	War Diary 18th Divisional Ammunition Column. R.F.A. March 1918		
War Diary	Rouez	01/03/1918	22/03/1918
War Diary	Rouez.	20/03/1918	20/03/1918
War Diary	Villequier-Aumont	22/03/1918	22/03/1918
War Diary	Bois De Caumont	22/03/1918	22/03/1918
War Diary	Bethancourt Grandru	23/03/1918	23/03/1918
War Diary	Porquericourt Pont L'Eveque Caisnes.	24/03/1918	24/03/1918
War Diary	Ribecourt. Caisnes. Pontoise	25/03/1918	25/03/1918
War Diary	Thurotte Caisnes Nampcel	26/03/1918	26/03/1918
War Diary	Haute Brave Caisnes	27/03/1918	27/03/1918
War Diary	Longueil-St Mairie. Area	31/03/1918	31/03/1918
War Diary	Liancourt Area	01/03/1918	01/04/1918
Heading	18th Divisional Ammunition Column. April 1918		
War Diary	Liancourt Area	01/04/1918	01/04/1918
War Diary	St Rimqult.	02/04/1918	02/04/1918
War Diary	Vief Villers	03/04/1918	03/04/1918
War Diary	Fresnoy-Au-Val	04/04/1918	04/04/1918
War Diary	Bussy-Le-Poix.	05/04/1918	05/04/1918
War Diary	Charny.	08/04/1918	08/04/1918
War Diary	Warlus	10/04/1918	10/04/1918
War Diary	Grandsart	11/04/1918	11/04/1918
War Diary	Rivery (Amiens)	15/04/1918	15/04/1918
War Diary	Boves	16/04/1918	16/04/1918
War Diary	St Ouen.	29/04/1918	03/05/1918
War Diary	Behencourt.	03/05/1918	31/05/1918
War Diary	St Ouen	01/05/1918	03/05/1918
War Diary	Behencourt	03/05/1918	31/05/1918
War Diary	St Ouen.	01/05/1918	03/05/1918
War Diary	Behencourt	03/05/1918	31/05/1918
War Diary	St Ouen	01/05/1918	03/05/1918
War Diary	Behencourt	03/05/1918	19/06/1918
War Diary	Area of Beaucourt	19/06/1918	30/06/1918
War Diary	Behencourt	01/06/1918	19/06/1918
War Diary	Beaucourt Area	19/06/1918	30/06/1918
War Diary	Behencourt	01/06/1918	19/06/1918
War Diary	Beaucourt Area	19/06/1918	30/06/1918
War Diary	Behencourt	01/06/1918	19/06/1918
War Diary	Beaucourt Area	19/06/1918	14/07/1918
War Diary	Longpre-Les-Amiens	14/07/1918	31/07/1918
War Diary	Beaucourt Area	01/07/1918	14/07/1918
War Diary	Longpre-Les Amiens	14/07/1918	31/07/1918
War Diary	Beaucourt.	01/07/1918	14/07/1918
War Diary	Longpre-Les-Amiens.	14/07/1918	14/07/1918
War Diary	Beaucourt Area	01/07/1918	14/07/1918
War Diary	Longpre-Les Amiens	14/07/1918	31/07/1918
Heading	18th Division. Artillery. 18th Divisional Ammunition Column R.F.A. August 1918		
War Diary	Longpre-Les Amiens.	01/08/1918	02/08/1918
War Diary	Frechencourt	02/08/1918	15/08/1918
War Diary	Heilly.	16/08/1918	27/08/1918
War Diary	Albert Area	28/08/1918	28/08/1918

War Diary	Fricourt Area	01/08/1918	31/08/1918
War Diary	Longpre-Les Amiens	01/08/1918	02/08/1918
War Diary	Frechencourt	02/08/1918	15/08/1918
War Diary	Heilly	16/08/1918	27/08/1918
War Diary	Albert Area	28/08/1918	28/08/1918
War Diary	Fricourt Area	31/08/1918	31/08/1918
War Diary	Longpre-Les-Amiens	01/08/1918	02/08/1918
War Diary	Frechencourt	02/08/1918	15/08/1918
War Diary	Heilly	16/08/1918	27/08/1918
War Diary	Albert Area	28/08/1918	28/08/1918
War Diary	Fricourt Area	31/08/1918	31/08/1918
War Diary	Longpre-Les Amiens	01/08/1918	02/08/1918
War Diary	Frechencourt	02/08/1918	15/08/1918
War Diary	Heilly	16/08/1918	27/08/1918
War Diary	Albert Area	28/08/1918	28/08/1918
War Diary	Fricourt Area	31/08/1918	31/08/1918
Miscellaneous	Headquarters 18 Div Arty Officer To RH & R.F.A. Records.	13/10/1918	13/10/1918
War Diary	Fricourt Area	01/08/1918	02/08/1918
War Diary	Trones Wood	02/08/1918	03/08/1918
War Diary	Maurepas	03/08/1918	16/08/1918
War Diary	Moislains	16/08/1918	30/08/1918
War Diary	Fricourt Area	01/08/1918	02/08/1918
War Diary	Trones Wood	02/08/1918	03/08/1918
War Diary	Maurepas	03/08/1918	16/08/1918
War Diary	Moislains	16/08/1918	30/08/1918
War Diary	Fricourt Area	01/08/1918	02/08/1918
War Diary	Trones Wood	02/08/1918	03/08/1918
War Diary	Maurepas	03/08/1918	16/08/1918
War Diary	Moislains	16/08/1918	30/08/1918
War Diary	Fricourt Area	01/08/1918	02/08/1918
War Diary	Trones Wood	02/08/1918	03/08/1918
War Diary	Maurepas	03/08/1918	16/08/1918
War Diary	Moislains	16/08/1918	30/08/1918
War Diary	Fricourt Area	01/08/1918	02/08/1918
War Diary	Trones Wood	02/08/1918	03/08/1918
War Diary	Maurepas	03/08/1918	16/08/1918
War Diary	Moislains	16/08/1918	30/08/1918
War Diary	Moislains	01/10/1918	03/10/1918
War Diary	Aizecourt Le Bas	03/10/1918	04/10/1918
War Diary	Saulcourt	04/10/1918	07/10/1918
War Diary	Bony	07/10/1918	09/10/1918
War Diary	Elincourt	09/10/1918	15/10/1918
War Diary	Avelu	15/10/1918	21/10/1918
War Diary	Maurois	21/10/1918	27/10/1918
War Diary	Le Cateau	27/10/1918	31/10/1918
War Diary	Moislains	01/10/1918	03/10/1918
War Diary	Aizecourt Le Bas	03/10/1918	04/10/1918
War Diary	Saulcourt	04/10/1918	07/10/1918
War Diary	Bony	07/10/1918	09/10/1918
War Diary	Elincourt	09/10/1918	15/10/1918
War Diary	Avelu	15/10/1918	21/10/1918
War Diary	Maurois	21/10/1918	27/10/1918
War Diary	Le Cateau	27/10/1918	31/10/1918
War Diary	Moislains	01/10/1918	03/10/1918
War Diary	Aizecourt-Le-Bas	03/10/1918	04/10/1918

War Diary	Saulcourt	04/10/1918	07/10/1918
War Diary	Bony	07/10/1918	09/10/1918
War Diary	Elincourt	09/10/1918	15/10/1918
War Diary	Avelu	15/10/1918	21/10/1918
War Diary	Maurois	21/10/1918	27/10/1918
War Diary	Le Cateau	27/10/1918	31/10/1918
War Diary	Le Cateau	01/11/1918	08/11/1918
War Diary	Maretz	08/11/1918	30/11/1918
War Diary	Le Cateau	01/11/1918	08/11/1918
War Diary	Maretz	08/11/1918	30/11/1918
War Diary	Le Cateau	01/11/1918	08/11/1918
War Diary	Maretz	08/11/1918	31/12/1918
War Diary	Maretz	01/12/1918	31/01/1919
War Diary	Maretz	01/03/1919	15/03/1919
War Diary	Mauliguy	15/03/1919	31/03/1919
War Diary	Maretz	01/03/1919	15/03/1919
War Diary	Mouliguy	15/03/1919	31/03/1919

No 95/2026/2

18TH DIVISION

18TH DIVL AMMN COL.
AUG 1915 - MAR 1919

Army Form C. 2118

WAR DIARY
or
INTELLIGENCE SUMMARY
(Erase heading not required.)

Instructions regarding War Diaries and Intelligence Summaries are contained in F.S. Regs., Part II. and the Staff Manual respectively. Title Pages will be prepared in manuscript.

Place	Date	Hour	Summary of Events and Information	Remarks and references to Appendices
HEYTESBURY	26/11	21.	1st Train Party left camp	
	27 "	0.55	1st Train left WARMINSTER Station	
	" "	8.	8. & last Train Party moved off.	
WARMIN-STER	" "	11	" " " left WARMINSTER.	
SOUTH-HAMPTON	" "	13	Last Train Party reached Southampton. 3 Transports for Column Head Qrs & Portion No 1 Section. Sailed on S.S. "AFRICAN PRINCE"	
LE HAVRE	28 "	17-30	Arrived 1/6 LE HAVRE. French interpreter joined	
MONTON-VILLERS	29	1	Column joined up at Montonvillers Night of 29/29 & camped in 2 Portion 1 Mule left at AMIENS lame in charge of Civilian 29/8/15. No 3 Secy	

BE

12/7517

18th Brown

18th Sikhs A.C.
Vol: I
Aug & Sep/15

Army Form C. 2118

WAR DIARY
or
INTELLIGENCE SUMMARY
(Erase heading not required.)

Instructions regarding War Diaries and Intelligence Summaries are contained in F.S. Regs., Part II. and the Staff Manual respectively. Title Pages will be prepared in manuscript.

Place	Date 1915	Hour	Summary of Events and Information	Remarks and references to Appendices
MONTONVIL-LERS	1. viii	3.00	Lt. E. MANLY admitted to Casualty Clearing Stn. VILLER BOCAGE. 1 Horse died (I Sec.) 1 Horse died (I Sec.).	Aug 4
	2 "	23.00	1 horse sent to casualty clearing Stn. Lt. E. MANLY discharged from Casualty Clearing Stn.	
	5 "			
	6 "	0.45	Orders recd. from H.Q. Div. Arty to move to BEAUCOURT (MAP AMIENS 12) at 6-30 on 7. viii. 15.	
	" "	23.45	Orders recd from H.Q. Div. Arty postponing move to BEAUCOURT for 24 Hours.	
	7 "	9.40	March Orders " " " received for " " "	
	8 "	4.00	Hd. Qrs, N°1 & N°3 Section Marched BEAUCOURT via VILLER BOCAGE and RAINVILLE. Met 85 Bgde R.F.A. at RAINVILLE Church and marched behind them to BEAUCOURT	
BEAUCOURT		8.00	Reached BEAUCOURT. 1 Horse left on road sick with Colic. by N°3 Section died about midnight.	
	11 "	22.00	Bvt. Maj. Gen. MAXSE. Com'dng XVIII Div. inspected 18th D.A.C.	
	12 "		1 Driver sent to Hospital at CORBIE. Recovered Mule left at AMIENS 1/8/15	
	17 "		1 Mule died N°3 Sec.	
	18 "		1 Horse died do.	
	23 "		A.D.M.S. 18th Div. and 18th Div. Arty. removed to HEILLY.	
	26 "	7.30	1 Milit. Suspect N°3 Section moved to BONNAY. 1 Driver Sent to Hospital. A Draft of 1 B.S.M, 2 Sergts, 3 Drivers & 2 Gunners arrived.	
	27 "		1 Sergt. Sent to 84th Brigade R.F.A. to replace Casualty	

Army Form C. 2118

WAR DIARY or **INTELLIGENCE SUMMARY**
(Erase heading not required.)

Instructions regarding War Diaries and Intelligence Summaries are contained in F.S. Regs., Part II. and the Staff Manual respectively. Title Pages will be prepared in manuscript.

Place	Date 1915	Hour	Summary of Events and Information	Remarks and references to Appendices
BONNAY	2&3/IX		1 L.D. Horses N° I Sec. Died	
	4 "		Sgt. Stewart sent to Hospital at CORBIE. N° II Sec. 1 L.D. Ht. M.V.S.	
	6 "		N° I Sec. lost 1 Mule (died).	
	14 "		S.S. Davey Sent to 55 Field Ambulance MERICOURT, Suspected Cerebro-Spinal - Meningitis. N° III lost 1 L.D.H.	
	20 "		D° H.S. Watts & Selwood Sent to 55 Field Ambulance MERICOURT Report received that S.S. Davey is not suffering from Cerebro-Spinal-be	
	23 "		D° Wright, Capt. Ede & D° Brown Sent to 55 Field Ambulance	
	"		D° Brown Sent back from 55 F.A.	
	24 "		Sgt. Dolan Sent to 55 Field Amb. a Boil. Brought to C.C.S. Villa Bocage	
	25 "		D° Anson to 55 F.A. at MERICOURT. 5 Horses to Mob. Vet. Section.	
	"		Received Secret Instructions re Proceedure in Case of an Advance.	
	27 "		" Report on Country between BAPAUME-PERONNE-ST QUENTIN-CAMBRAI	
	29 "		D° S. Strahan Sent to 55 F.A. MERICOURT.	
	30 "		N° 3 Section Sent 2 Horses to Mobile Vet. Section. gr.	
	"		1 anderit Sent to Hospital.	

121/7593

18th Hussain

18th B.A.P.
Vol 2
Oct 15

WAR DIARY or INTELLIGENCE SUMMARY

Army Form C. 2118

Place	Date 1915	Hour	Summary of Events and Information	Remarks and references to Appendices
BONNAY	Oct. 1		1 Riding Horse sent to Mob. Vet. Sec.	
	" 2		5 L.A. Horses & 4 Mules Received. Dr W. Pomfrey B.H. Hospital	
	" 4		1 L.D. Horse & 1 Mule Sent to Mob. Vet. Section. Dr F. Brandeny to Hospital	
	" 3		S/S Looker, A.S.M.T. B.H. Hospital	
	" 4	9.10 A.M	Dr Davise, E.C. accidentally killed	
	" 5		1 L.A. Horse to Mob. Vet. Section. Dr Hicks dischd. Hosp!	
	" 7		3 to " "	
	" 8		Broadway	
	" 11		S.S. Loggers from Div'l Rest	
	" 12		3 L.D. Horses received.	
	" 18		Sn. J. Adair & Dr A.L. Shaw to Base Depot	
			Sno. Watts & D. V. admit to England. 1 L.D. Horse & 1 Mule to Mob. Vet. Sec.	
	" 20		Officer Change dud.	
	" 21		1 L.A. Horse to Mob. Vet. Sec. § Dr Broadway evacuated from Area 4 Horses & 2 Mules Rec'd	
	" 22		1 L.D. Horse discd. " S Cutler " Base Depot " "	
	" 23		Cold shoer Hickford to N°2 Gen. Base Depot	
	" 25		1 Mule to Mob. Vet. Sec.	
	" 26		A/S.J. holding admitted Hospital	
			D. A. Silmour evacuated from Area	

WAR DIARY
or
INTELLIGENCE SUMMARY

Army Form C. 2118

Place	Date	Hour	Summary of Events and Information	Remarks and references to Appendices
BONNAY	26 Oct		2 L.D. Horses to Mot. Vet. Section	
	27 "		2 Do. Do. Do. Do.	
	31 "		1 L.D. Horse & 1 Mule Do. Do. Do.	

Major John Lt. Col.
Comdg. Div. Amm. Col.
XVIII Div.

18th Sept.
Vol 3

7734/D/

18th Kurram

Nov 15

WAR DIARY
or
INTELLIGENCE SUMMARY

Army Form C. 2118

Place	Date	Hour	Summary of Events and Information	Remarks and references to Appendices
BONNAY	11/11			
	12/11		Capt. RISLEY joined from Base. Transfer 6 Drivers to 82nd B.A.C.	
			2 Gunners 1 " " 83rd "	
			2 Bombrs 1 " " 84th "	
			1 Gunner 1 " " 85th "	
	13/11		2 Lieut. C.W.K. WHITE joined on posting from Base.	
	16/11		1 Acting Gunner Lieut. joined to	
	17/11		1 A.V.C. Sergt. to 119 H. Bty. R.G.A.	
			2 Lieut C.W.K. WHITE to 82nd Bde R.F.A.	
			2 Lieut. FRASER to 84th "	
	18/11		1 QMS. and 3 Gunners from Base.	
	21/11		2 Gunners + 5 Gunners transferred to Bde. 1 F.D. Horse discharged	
	23/11		1 to hospital. 1 B. + 5 Gunners from Base.	
			12 men attached from Brigade a/t. for telephone employ from Base.	
	24/11		1 Dr. to to 5 Gunners transferred from Base.	
	24/11		men to Streets. Twenty men 1 Mills + Ashton	
			Capt. Lorne B. A.D.S.S.	
	29/11		1 N.B.S. Dr. transferred to 18. A.S.P. 1 Dr. to 18 A.C. from 18 A.S.P	

Army Form C. 2

WAR DIARY
or
INTELLIGENCE SUMMARY
(Erase heading not required.)

Instructions regarding War Diaries and Intelligence Summaries are contained in F. S. Regs., Part II. and the Staff Manual respectively. Title Pages will be prepared in manuscript.

Place	Date	Hour	Summary of Events and Information	Remarks and references to Appendices
BONNAY	20 Nov		1 L.D. Horse died.	
	25 "		Sr. evacuated upon age.	
	26 "		1 L.D. Horse destroyed	
			2 Ambl. 1 S/Smith 12 D. mules & 9 h mules posted from B xx	
			Transfer 4 D. mules to 82 D.A.C.	
			1 Ambl. + 2 D. mules to 83rd D.A.C.	
			1 Bomb. " " 84th "	
			4 D. mules + 3 h mules 85th "	
	28 "		9 h mules, 1 trumpeter & driver from B.A.C. S 201	
			3 drivers to telephone exchange.	
			1 Driver to Hospital	
	29 "		2 S/Sgts. 13 h mules + 23 D. mules posted from B xx Depot	

For Vet. Hosp Lt. Col
D.A.C. " 18 " "
Dec /1915

Army Form C. 2118

WAR DIARY
or
INTELLIGENCE SUMMARY
(Erase heading not required.)

Instructions regarding War Diaries and Intelligence Summaries are contained in F.S. Regs., Part II. and the Staff Manual respectively. Title Pages will be prepared in manuscript.

Place	Date	Hour	Summary of Events and Information	Remarks and references to Appendices
BONNAY	Nov. 1		Gr. Simpson to No 2 Gen. Base Depot	
	"2		1 Mule destroyed	
	"3		Dr W. Cobley & W. Pomfrey, Dr R. Salisbury & Dr. T. Bragger evacuated from Area.	
			Dr. F. Rog accidentally killed	
	"4		Dr. J. Davis to Hospital	
	"5		Dr. T. Bragger to No 2 Gen. Base Depot	1 C. 5I.D
			Horses & 3 Mules received from Remounts.	Corpl.
			Lc. Kenzie & A/c Witham to Hospital	
			No 5926 & A/c J. Ward absent without leave & returned to A.P.M.	
	"6		A/c W. Cape to Hospital.	1. L.A. Horse destroyed.
	"7		A/cs Millet, Ponting, W. Sharp, F., Amarks J., McCormack, Franchetti F., & Davis B.F. posted from No 2 Gen. Base Depot, Havre.
	"8		A/cs Boyd F. S.S. Turner C., Dr R. Thwell S. & Higgs H., & Jr. & Gill W., White W. & Rhoesome S.H., transferred to 83rd Bgd RFA.
			16 + Mules sent to 26th Division.	
	"9		A/cs Witham J. & Cape W. evacuated from Div. Area.	

1875 Wt. W593/826 1,000,000 4/15 J.B.C. & A. A.D.S.S./Forms/C. 2118.

18th Kurram

18th Sept.
Vol: 4

121/7809

Recd 15

Confidential

WAR DIARY
or
INTELLIGENCE SUMMARY
(Erase heading not required.)

Army Form C. 2118

Div. AMM. COLUMN
18th DIVISION

Instructions regarding War Diaries and Intelligence Summaries are contained in F.S. Regs., Part II. and the Staff Manual respectively. Title Pages will be prepared in manuscript.

Place	Date	Hour	Summary of Events and Information	Remarks and references to Appendices
BONNAY	Dec. 1		Lieut O'Keefe posted from Base Depot	
	2		1 Driver posted from Base Depot	
	3		1 Gunner " " "	
			6 Gunners & Drivers posted to 82nd Brigade R.F.A.	
	5		" " " 83rd " "	
			" " " 84th " "	
			" " " 83rd " "	
	4		1 Driver to Hospital	
			1 " " "	
			1 " " "	
	4		1 " " "	
			2 Lieuts. C.O. KITCHENER, J. INVERARITY & R.S. DAVEY posted to Column	
			1 Driver to Hospital. 1 Driver discharged from hospital	
			Lieut. R HEWER posted to 84th Brigade R.F.A.	
			Lieut. T. TWENTYMAN " " 82nd " "	
			1 Driver from Hospital	
			1 B. 1 Gunner & 1 Driver from Base Depot	
			1 Mule destroyed. 1 Mule to M.V. Section.	

WAR DIARY
or
INTELLIGENCE SUMMARY
(Erase heading not required.)

Army Form C. 2118

DIV. AMM. COLUMN
18th DIVISION.

Place	Date	Hour	Summary of Events and Information	Remarks and references to Appendices
BONNAY	1915 17 Dec		4 Gunner & 1 Driver to 83rd Bng. R.F.A.	
	18		do " " 4 " " "	
	"		" " 1 " " "	
	"		Cont.	
	"		1 Gunner to Ammunition Column re-join 1st Army	
	19		1 Gunner to Hospital	
	20		1 Gunner & 1 Driver wounded from Aerm.	
	21		1 Gunner to Hospital. 1 Driver from Hospital. 1 Driver joined from Base 83rd Bng. R.F.A.
	22		LIEUT. J.B. NEVILLE posted to 83rd Bng. R.F.A. Dept.
	23		1 Driver to 83rd Bng. R.F.A. 1 Cpl. to Trench Mortar School
	24		3 Gunners " " " 83rd " "	
	"		6 " " " 84th " "	
	"		4 " " " 83rd " "	
	"		2 " " " 84th " "	
	"		3 " " " 85th " "	
	25		No 2 Section ordered to proceed to BUIRE this day	
	"		1 Gunner from Hospital. 4 TD Horses to M.V Section. 3 Horses to Anti-aircraft Section
	"		1 Driver from "	
	26		1 Gunner to Hospital	
	27		1 Gunner to 82nd Brigade R.F.A. 1 Driver to 83rd Bng. R.F.A.	
	31		4 Gunners & 4 Drivers to 85th Bng. R.F.A	

85ᵗᵉ Bde. A.C.
Vol: 6
Tamil

Army Form C. 2118.

WAR DIARY
or
INTELLIGENCE SUMMARY.
(Erase heading not required.)

85th Brigade Ammunition Column RFA

Month of January 16

Place	Date	Hour	Summary of Events and Information	Remarks and references to Appendices
TREUX	1.1.16		Still at TREUX	
	14.1.16		Capt J.G. Houghton evacuated to AMIENS	
	20.1.16		D Subsection reformed Column	
	21.1.16		Capt W.S. Webster joined from D/82 RFA to Command Column	
	22.1.16 to 31.1.16		Still at TREUX	

Officers { 85th BAC
Capt W.S. Webster
Lt. E.C. Sylvester

M. Webster
Capt 85 BAC

WAR DIARY
or
INTELLIGENCE SUMMARY
(Erase heading not required.)

Army Form C. 2118

Div. Amm. Column
1st Division

Place	Date 1916	Hour	Summary of Events and Information	Remarks and references to Appendices
BONNAY	Jan. 1		2 Drivers + 1 Saddler to Hospital	
	" 2		1 " " + 1 Saddler from Hospital	
	" 4		3 men Rec. Depot & returning to 1B. 1 E.A. Horse & 5 Mule from Remounts	
	" 5		Driver to Hospital. 2 Drivers from Hospital	
	" 6		Driver from Hospital	
	" 7		1 gunner + 2 Drivers transferred to 83rd Brig. R.F.A.	
	" 8		" " " " 84	
	" "		" " " " 85	
	" "		2 " " " 3 " " " 83	
	" "		3 " " " " " " 82	1 Dr from Hospital
	" 9		2 Lt. D. Ashton	
	" "		2 Lt. H. O'Keefe	
	" "		2 Lt. E.O. Kitchener	
	" 10		1 L.D. Horse to M.V. Section	
	" "		1 E.A. Horse to M.V. Section. 1 Driver to Hospital	
	" 12		2 gunners + 10 Drivers from B wae. 1 Mule to M.V. Section.	
	" 13		" " to Hospital.	
	" 14		4 " " from Bmce	
	" 15		1 Gr. to Hospital. 2 gunners from Hospital. 1 D. Horse died	
			Transfer. 1 Driver to 82nd Brigade	
			1 gunner " 82 "	
			1 " " 83 "	

WAR DIARY
INTELLIGENCE SUMMARY

Army Form C. 2118

Dw. Amm. Colum
18th Division

Place	Date	Hour	Summary of Events and Information	Remarks and references to Appendices
BONNAY	Jan 15th		Transfer 2 Gunners to 84th Brigade	
"	"		3 " + 2 Drivers " 85th "	
"	"	18	1 Gunner to Hospital	
"	"	19	1 Gunner from Hospital	
"	"	20	1 D.A.C. Driver from Base	
"	"	21	1 Driver to Hospital	
"	"		3 L.A.D. Horses (evacuated when on tram to 51st D. W. but not reported)	
"	"		Officers Posted from Base :— Lieut C. P. Lait 2/Lt B. B. Trowbridge	
"	"		2/Lt W. B. Fletcher. 1 Driver to 82nd Bde R.F.A. 3 Gunners to Rgmt. 2 Drivers to 84th Bde. 1 Driver to 85th Bde.	
"	"		83rd Ammn Column Bombing & Lt. L. H. Trimby posted from Base	
"	"	22	A. & S.E. Machine from Base	
"	"		4 Drivers to Hospital. 1 L.A.D. Horse to M.V. Section	Recd
"	"	23	1 Gunner from Hospital. 1 Gunner to Brig. R.F.A. 3 Driver to Hospital. 5 Remounts	
"	"	24	A. & g. L. Ellis to B. 2nd Brig. R.F.A. 1 Gunner from Hospital	
"	"	25	Home to M.V. Section	
"	"	26	1 Gunner from Base. 1 Ammn Hospital. Brig. R.F.A.	
"	"	27	1 Driver to 82nd " "	
"	"	"	— " 83rd " "	
"	"	"	— " 84th " "	
"	"	"	— " 85th " "	
"	"	28	1 Gunner + 2 Drivers. 2 L.A.D. Horses to M.V. Section	
"	"	30	1 S/Smith discharged from Hospital	

A.D.S./Forms C. 2118.

85th Bde Ammn Column

Vol VII

A.C.C. 2H

From O.C.
    85th Bty, Amm Column
      R.F.A

To Officer i/c
   A.G's Office at the
      Base.

    Attached please find War Diary of this Unit for February 1916

1/3/16

          [signature] R.F.A
     Commanding Ammunition Column 85 Bde R.F.A

Army Form C. 2118.

WAR DIARY
or
INTELLIGENCE SUMMARY.
(Erase heading not required.)

Instructions regarding War Diaries and Intelligence Summaries are contained in F. S. Regs., Part II. and the Staff Manual respectively. Title pages will be prepared in manuscript.

Place	Date	Hour	Summary of Events and Information	Remarks and references to Appendices
TREUX	1.2.16			
LAVIÉVILLE	6.2.16		Column moved to LAVIÉVILLE	
"	8.2.16		"B" Subsection Strength 19 NCOs & men, 36 Horses, 4 Ammunition Wagons. Transference to B Battery 85th Bde RFA on the Transfer of this Battery to 35th Division (A/85 RFA)	
"	13.2.16		2/Lt L.H. Twinby joined from A/85 RFA	
"	29.2.16		Column still at LAVIÉVILLE	
			Officers of 85th BAC	
			Capt W.S. Webster	
			2/Lt E.C. Sylvester	
			" L.H. Twinby	

29/16

W. Nicholls Talbot
Cmdg 85th BAC.

18th Dec 3
Comm Pot
ng

WAR DIARY
or
INTELLIGENCE SUMMARY
(Erase heading not required.)

Army Form C. 2118

29.3.16

Div. Amm. Column
18th Division

Place	Date	Hour	Summary of Events and Information	Remarks and references to Appendices
BONNAY	Feb 2		1 L.D. Horse sick. 1 Dr. to Hospital	
	" 3		4 Drivers from Bse. 1 Drum to Hospital. 5 Gnrs + 1 Dr from Base	
	" 4		A move to Hospital. Remounts Rec'd. 3R. 7 L.D.	
	" 5		" " "	
	" 6		Column moved. 2 Ammn Evacuated. 1 R.d + 2 L.D.H. over to M.V. Section	
	" 7		1 L.D. Horse died. 4 L.D. Horse to M.V. Section.	
	" 8		2 Lt. H.H. Goddy L.H. TRIM BY posted to 85th Bry. R.F.A	
PONT NOYELLE	" 10		1 hrs. transferred to 82nd Bry R.F.A	
	" 11		2 " " 83rd " "	
	" 12		3 Gnr + 4 Dro. " " Base. 1 B.S.M. from A/85 Brig. R.F.A	
	" 13		4 Gnr + 10 Dro. from M.V. Section	
	" 14		1 L.Cpl. H. Gpr th. Mule to Hospital. 1 Driver from C/55 " "	
	" 15		1 S/Smith to Hospital. 1 Driver from 3/2 East Anglian Bgd. & for attached left group	
	" 16		2 Lt. M.H. GODLEY to Hospital	
	" 17		Driver to Hospital. Remounts Rec'd. 2 Rd. 7 L.D.	
	" 18		Gunner to Hospital	83rd Brig. R.F.A
	" 19		1 Ammn to " " 85th " "	
	" 20		" " + 2 "	
	" 21		A mn to Hospital. 2 Lt. R.S. BOWMAN posted & attached B/83 Bgd.	
	" 22		3 L.D. Horse to M.V. Section. 1 Gunner to Hospital	83rd Bgd. R.F.A
	" 23		6 L.D. Horse " " "	
	" 24		1 S/Smith, 1 mlr, +10 Ammn from Base	
	" 25		1 Gr + 3 Drs. to 82 Bgd. 1 Dr. to B/84. 2 Dro + 2 Gyr. to 84th. 1 wheeler to 85th	
	" 27		1 B.S.M. to Hospital 1 L.D. Horse F.M. V. A. Section	

WAR DIARY
or
INTELLIGENCE SUMMARY
(Erase heading not required.)

Army Form C. 2118

Div. Amm. Column
18th Division

Place	Date	Hour	Summary of Events and Information	Remarks and references to Appendices
BONNAY	Feb 3		1 L.D. Horse died. 1 Driver transferred. 3 Gnr + 1 Dr from B. War	
	" 4		4 Drivers from B.gen. 1 Drivers to Hospital. Remounts recd. 3 R. 7 L.D.	
	" 5		1 Driver to Hospital	
PONT NOYELLE	" 6		Column moved. 2 Drivers Evacuated. 1 Rdr + 2 L.D.H over to M.V. Section	
	" 8		1 L.D. Horse died. 4 L.D. Horses to M.V. Section.	
	" 9		2 Rtr. F. H. H. Smith & Lt. H. TRIMBY posted to 85th Bdy R.F.A.	
	" 10		1 hfr. transferred to 82nd Bdy. R.F.A.	
	" 11		2 Dr. " " 83rd "	
	" 12		3 Dr. + 4 Dr. " " 84th "	
	" 13		4 Sgt + 10 Drs. from B.nee. 1 B.S.M. from A/75 Bdy R.F.A.	
	" 16		1 L.D. Horse + 1 Mule to M.V. Section. 1 Driver from C/75 " "	
	" 17		1/Smith to Hospital. 3/L Foot Anglican Regt. temp attached left from	
	" 18		1 H.M.H. Goodday, from 3/L Foot Anglian Regt. temp attached left from	
	" 19		1 Driver to Hospital	
	" "		1 Gunner to Hospital. Remounts recd: 2 Rd. 7 L.D.	
	" "		" + 1 Driver to 83 M. Bdy. R.F.A.	
	" "		" + 2 " 85th " "	
	" 22		1 Driver to Hospital. 1 Lt. R.S. BOWMAN posted + attached B/83 Bdy by	
	" 23		3 E.A. Horse to M.V.t. Section. 1 Gunner to Hospital	
	" 24		6 L.D. Horses to " "	
	" 25		1 S/Smith, 1 Bomb + 10 Drivers from B. gen	
	" 26		1 Sgt + 3 Drs. to 82 Bgde. 1 Dr. to 74th. 2 Drs + 2 Gr. 74th. 1 wheeler to 85	
	" 27		1 B.S.M. to Hospital. 1 L.D. Horse to M. V.t. Section.	

18 D3
A. Col
Vol 7

WAR DIARY
or
INTELLIGENCE SUMMARY
(Erase heading not required.)

Army Form C. 2118

18th Div. Ammn Column R.F.A.

Place	Date	Hour	Summary of Events and Information	Remarks and references to Appendices
PONT NOYELLE	March 1		2 L.D. Horses to Mob. Vet. Section	
	" 2		9 Gunners from Base	
	" 3		Driver to Hospital (L.D. Horse to Mob Vet Section)	
	" 5		1 L.D. Horse Died	
	" 6		1 R.+ 1 L.D. Horse + 1 Mule lost. Column moved to Bussy Les Douves	
BUSSY LES DOURS	" 7		1 L.D. Horse destroyed	
	" 9		2 Bro. 8 gns + 11 Drivers from Base	
	" 10		3 Drivers + 1 Gunner to Hospital from Base	
			1 Bro. 1 gn + 4 Drivers to 82nd Brig. R.F.A	
			1 " 1 " + 3 " " 83 " "	
			2 " " + " " 84 " "	
			3 " " + " " 85 " "	
	" 15		3 Drivers + 1 gn. from Hospital	
			1 gn. + 7 Drivers to 85 Brig. Driver evacuated. 1 L.D. Horse & Mob Vet Sect.	
	" 17		10 gns + 14 Drivers from Base.	
	" 19		2 A.S.P. Fatigues to 85th Brigade R.F.A. 12 Mules from A amounts	
			W.A. FLETCHER 83rd " "	
			R.A. CLARK " "	
			F.J. BARKER 82 " "	
			S.E. BACHUS " "	
			R.S. BOWMAN 84 " "	
			1 L.D H. one destroyed. 1 gn to 18 A.S.P 1 gn from 17th A.S.P	

WAR DIARY
or
INTELLIGENCE SUMMARY

Army Form C. 2118

7th Div. Amm. Column
18th Div. Amm. Column

Place	Date	Hour	Summary of Events and Information	Remarks and references to Appendices
BUSSY LES DOURS	May 1916 20		R. Capt. Conolly R.A.M.C. from No 3 Gen Base Hospital 2 Lpls + 5 Dvrs. to 84th Bry. A.F.A. 3 " " " " 84 " " 2 " " " " 84 " " 1 L.D.H. one died	
CHIPILLY	23		Column moved to CHIPILLY. 2 Sept 10 Cor. 14 kyo. 17 Drivers from Base 2 Sgts. 1 Lpl + 2 Dvrs. to 84 Bry R.F.A. Br. " " 1 " + 3 " " 82 " " S/Smith F. to Hospital	
	25		1 Driver to " Dis. to Hospital	
	F 28		3 Horses + 7 mules from Remount. 1 mule destroyed	
	25		18 Horses + 3 Wagons transferred to M.T. Depôt	
	30		1 Gr. evacuated	

Arres John
Comdg 18 D.A.C.
18th D.A.C. A C

85 Bde
Amm C
Vol 8

Army Form C. 2118.

WAR DIARY
or
INTELLIGENCE SUMMARY
(Erase heading not required.)

Instructions regarding War Diaries and Intelligence
Summaries are contained in F. S. Regs., Part II.
and the Staff Manual respectively. Title Pages
will be prepared in manuscript.

Place	Date	Hour	Summary of Events and Information	Remarks and references to Appendices
LAVIEVILLE	1/7/16		Column billeted here until 3rd inst.	
BUSSY LES DAOURS	3/7/16	9.30 pm	Moved to BUSSY LES DAOURS arrived at 2.0 pm.	
BOIS DES TAILLES	9/7/16	9.30 am	Moved to BOIS DES TAILLES arrived 2.30 pm.	
"	11/7/16		Lieut L.H. Ellsworth R.H.A. att.d for duty from 83rd Bde H.Q.rs	
"	23/7/16		Lieut L.H. Ellsworth M.V.C. left for England on completion of his contract of 1 year	
"	26/7/16		Lieut T. O'Connor M.V.C. joined in relief of Lieut L.H. Ellsworth	
"	31/7/16		Right Section moved to BOIS GRESSAIRE left section still in BOIS DES TAILLES	

Strength 1 S/S A. B.V.C.
Capt. W.S. Wright R.A.M
Lieut E.C. Edwards R.A.M
" L.H. Tranbery R.A.M
" T.O. O'Connor M.V.C (att.d)

W. Wright Capt R.A.M.
O in C A B.V.C

31/7/16

WAR DIARY or INTELLIGENCE SUMMARY

Army Form C. 2118

18th Div. Amm. Column VOL 8

(Erase heading not required.)

Place	Date 1916	Hour	Summary of Events and Information	Remarks and references to Appendices
CHIPILLY	April 1		1 L.D. Horse to Mob. Vet. Section	
	" 2		3 Saddlers + 5 Drivers from Base. 1 L.D. Horse from Mob. Vet. Sect.	
	" 3		1 Driver to Hospital	
	" 5		1 Gr. to 82 Brig. 1 fit. to 83rd Brig. + 2 Gnrs + 2 Drs. to 84th Brig. R.F.A.	
	" 7		5 L.D. Horses to Mob. Vet. Sec.	
	" 12		1 Dr. to Hospital. 1 L.D. Horse lost	
	" 13		1 Dr. evacuated.	
	" 15		1 " " to Hospital	
	" 17		1 " " discharged from Hospital. 1 L.D. Horse to M.V. Section	
	" 18		1 " " evacuated to Hospital. 1 L.D. Horse destroyed	
	" 19		5 Other Ranks from Base + 1 Dr. from Hospital	
	" 21		Dr. discharged from Hospital	
	" 22		5 Gunners from Base + 1 Dr. to Hospital	
	" 23		5 men to Hospital. 1 Dr. discharged from Hospital	
	" 25		1 " from Base	
	" 26		Dro.	
	" 28		Capt. Connelly R.A.M.C. to X111 Corps. Lt Kennedy posted + arrived. Lt. Johnson Lt-Col. O.C. 18 D.A.C.	

XVIII / vol 9
AC/86 RFA

Army Form C. 2118.

WAR DIARY
or
INTELLIGENCE SUMMARY.
(Erase heading not required.)

Place	Date	Hour	Summary of Events and Information	Remarks and references to Appendices
BOIS GRESSAIRE	1/4/16		Left Rechin moved to BOIS GRESSAIRE	
	2/4/16		2/Lt C.P. Laid RFA att'd to C/85 RFA from C/85 RFA	
			Mr E.C. Sylvester RFA att'd to C/85 RFA	
	30/4/16		Still in BOIS GRESSAIRE. Lt T. O'Connor att'd to D/85 RFA. M.Y.B. Keynes att'd from D/85 RFA	
			Officers of 85th BAC.	
			Capt W.S. Webster RFA	
			2/Lt C.P. Laid RFA	
			" L.H. Trumby RFA	
			" Y.B. Keynes RFA	
			30/4/16	
				Walsh Capt RFA
				Cmdg 85th BAC

Vol 9

Army Form C. 2118

WAR DIARY
or
INTELLIGENCE SUMMARY 18th. Div. Amm. Column
(Erase heading not required.)

Instructions regarding War Diaries and Intelligence Summaries are contained in F.S. Regs., Part II. and the Staff Manual respectively. Title Pages will be prepared in manuscript.

Place	Date	Hour	Summary of Events and Information	Remarks and references to Appendices
CHIPILLY	May 3		1 Sgt. to Hospital	
	4		1 Gunner from Base. 1 Admitt. Evacuated. 1 L.D. Hunt M.C. Vet. Sec.	
	5		3. 82nd Bry. R.F.A. 1 h.r. 12 Div. 1 251st Bry. R.F.A. Gyr. S Div.	
	6		1 Dr. to Hospital	
	7		1 Dvr. to Hospital. Column moved to ARGOEUVES	
ARGOEUVES	8		1 Lieut. + 1 other to Hospital	
	9		15 O.R. + 14 Drs. from Base. 2 L.D. Horses to M.b. Vet. Sec.	
	11		2 L.D. Horses + 1 R. Horse to M.b. Vet. Sec. 3	
	12		L.D. Horses to 251st Bry. R.F.A. 13 h.r. + 5 Div. T., 24th Bry. R.F.A.	
	13		1 Sgt. + 2 Drs. evacuated. 1 Sth Dr. discharged from Hospital	
	15		A.A.C. brought up to war establishment.	
	17		1 Dvr. to Hospital	
	19		1 Sgt. + 1 Dvr. to Hospital	
	21		Dr. to Hospital.	
	25		Lt. ASHBY Tr. 84th Bry. R.F.A. Lt. KENNEDY R.A.M.C. Tr. XII F.Amb.Cas. Lt. REYNES. 2.Lait L.D.A.C.+ A. DAVEY to W/o H.T.M.B.[?] 1 Dvr. entry. lt. Hospital	
	26		1 Sgt. from Hospital. 1 Dr. to Hospital	
	27		1 Dvr.	

CONFIDENTIAL

From OC
21st Bde Amm Col
Details

To: officer i/c
C.B. Office at the Base

May 23rd/16

Herewith War Diary for
the month of May 16

[signature]
Capt RFA
OC 21st Bde AC RFA Details

85 Brigade
RFA A e

1 P Div

Vol 10

WAR DIARY or INTELLIGENCE SUMMARY.

Army Form C. 2118

(Erase heading not required.)

Place	Date	Hour	Summary of Events and Information	Remarks and references to Appendices
BOIS GRESSAIRE	15/3/16		9th in BOIS GRESSAIRE	
	16/3/16		2/Lt LUTTMAN posted to A/85 RFA	
			" E.C. SYLVESTER posted to C/85 RFA	
			2/Lt T.B. KEYMS posted to 83rd B.A.C. from A/85 RFA	
			83rd B.A.C. demobilized	
			2 Gunners & Drivers 6 LD Horses 1 GS wagon to 83rd B HQ	
			6 Gunners 13 Drivers 27 LD Horses 2 Amn Wagons to 82nd BAC	
			5 " 13 " 27 " 4 " " 83rd BAC	
			5 " 13 " 27 " 4 " " 84th BAC	
			3 Officers 1 MGO (2nd Cl) 25 Other Ranks 11 RI Horses 1 GS Wagon provided	
	17/3/16		DETAILS (commanded by Capt FAIRLIE RFA) at ARGOEUVES	
			Officers in Glenum at time of demobilization	
			Capt W.S. Webster RFA Commanding	
			2nd Lt CP Earl RFA	
			" T.B. Keyms RFA	

WAR DIARY

INTELLIGENCE SUMMARY 18th Div. AMM COLUMN R.F.A.

Army Form C. 2118

(Erase heading not required.)

Place	Date	Hour	Summary of Events and Information	Remarks and references to Appendices
ARGOEUVES	JUN -1 1916		1 Dr. discharged from Hospital 1 L.D. Horse Lost	
"	5		1 L.D. Horse Died	
"	8		A.A. Horse received from Remount	
"	9		A.A. + Sgt. admitted to Hospital 1 L.D. Horse killed	
"	10		A.A. admitted to Hospital	
"	11		1 L.D. Horse evacuated. Column moved to GROVETOWN	
GROVETOWN CAMP	11		Sgt. + 1 Dr. to Hospital 1 D². died on the March.	
"	"		H.Q. arrived at GROVETOWN CAMP + N°s 2 + 3 Sections Bois des TAILLES	
"	13		Scout cycle went for instructions. Received from Div. Staff	
"	14		1 B/. to Hospital 1 Gr. from Hospital 2 L.D. Horses + 1 Mule from Remounts 2 L.D. Horses to Mob. Vet. Section 3 Mules from Base	
"			1 B/. 3 Lt. R.A.H.H. N°. 1/1x6 received giving details administrative instructions for forthcoming operations on Div. front	
"	15		R.A.H.H. 352 instructions as to infantry carrying parties received 1 B/. Hospital 1 L.D. Horse died 4 Gr. + 2 Dr. to 83rd Brig. 4 Dr. to F.B. 4 Brig. 4 Gr. + 3 drivers F.T.S. to Brig.	

Army Form C. 2118

WAR DIARY
or
INTELLIGENCE SUMMARY

18th D.A.C.

(Erase heading not required.)

Instructions regarding War Diaries and Intelligence Summaries are contained in F. S. Regs., Part II. and the Staff Manual respectively. Title Pages will be prepared in manuscript.

Place	Date	Hour	Summary of Events and Information	Remarks and references to Appendices
GROVETOWN CAMP	Jan 16		1 Dr + 1 Sergt from Hospital. 1 L.D. Horse Killed. 2Lt. PLATTS to 84th Bty	
	" 17		H.Q. to BOIS DÉSTAILLES. 1 Dr. from Hospital.	
			4 L.D. Horses + 1 Mule Killed. 4 L.D. Horses + 1 Mule to M.L. Vet. Sec.	
			A personal Armoured D. runt at K. 18 d. 4. 2. has 62 ♃ horses N.E.	
			Placed under charge of O.C. 18 D.A.C. Ammns brought up	
			by A.S.P. lorries + dumped at side of Road + waybills filled	
GROVETOWN CAMP			by other side of Dump taken up to the line at Night	
	" 19		1 B.S.M (N/17 H.T. N.3) to Hospital. 1 Dr Killed in action	
			1 Mule to Mob. Vet sect.	
	" 20		3 Dr's wounded (in action) + to Hospital. 1 Corpl + 2 Bombrs.	
			from line. 1 Mule to Mob. Vet Sec". Administrative Ammuniments to H.A. 1/126	
	" 21		1 Dr. to Hospital. Administrative Ammuniments.	
	" 22		1 Mule to Mob. Vet Sec". Administrative	
			Ammuniments + Supplementary Instructions to H.A. 1/126	
			received.	
	" 23		1 Dr from Hospital	

Army Form C. 2118

WAR DIARY
or
INTELLIGENCE SUMMARY
(Erase heading not required.)

18th D A C

Place	Date	Hour	Summary of Events and Information	Remarks and references to Appendices
BOIS DES TAILLES	July 25		Operations are said to have commenced on our front. 1 B. & S. M. to Hospital & kramated.	
			A.V. to Hospital. Administrative Instructions No. 3. Q.P.37/3 received.	
	26		Sent back to Sally le Sec (5 mls behind A R P) B.Ech. discharged from Hospital. 1 L D Horses to M.L. Vet.Sec	
	27		1 L.D. to Hospital. 1 R + 3 L D Horses to 83rd Brig.	
			1 L D to 8th 85th Brig. 1 R to 85th Brig. 1 L D killed	
			1 L A to Mt. Vet. Sectn. 1 B.S.M. 1 Br. 1 Sgt.	
			1 L A + 1 Dr. from Base. 1 B.S.M. to 84th Brig.	
	28		1 R + 1 L D 2 mls from Rhumont. 1 Sgt + 1 Dr. to 83rd Brig in	
			Chauns to 2 Brig. 1 Sgt + 1 Dr. to 83rd Brig in	
			9 Sth to 8 + 85th Brig. 1 Sgt + 1 Dr. to 85 Brig.	
			5 Gunners from Base.	
	29		Hostility 3 L D Horses to M.L. Vet Sec	
			+ forth + 3 from Brevel. 1 L D Horse to	
			R. Horse + 4 Gers to 83rd Brig. 1 L D Horse to	
	30		1 L D Horse to the T 85 Brig	Aug 5

18th Divn. Ammunition Column

WAR DIARY
or
INTELLIGENCE SUMMARY   18th D.A.C.

(Erase heading not required.)

Army Form C. 2118

Place	Date 1916	Hour	Summary of Events and Information	Remarks and references to Appendices
H.Q. Central (Maria 12 D.)	July 1		1 Off. & 2 A.R. to 83rd Brig. R.F.A.	
	2		1 L.D. Horse to 84th Brig.	
	3		1 Sergt. A.V.C. opr (attd.) to Hospital. 1 L.D. Horse to 84th Brig.	
	4		1 L.D. Horse to Mob. Vet. Sec. XIII Corps N.Z. R Sie. (Instructions)	
			2 9m (Springs) recd.	
	5		1 Sergt. A.V.C. died in Hospital. 1 R. & 5 L.D. to 85th Brig.	
			1 Mule to 82nd Brig. 1 L.D. Horse to M.V. Sec.	
	6		10 Offs. & 5 Mules to 81st Brig. 4 L.D. Horses to 82nd Brig.	
			1 L.D. Horse to M.V. Sec. Lt. W.H. Horne to 85th Brig.	
			2 Lieut. E. ISMAY & W.R. CRUIKSHANK from B ac.	
			1 L.D. Horse to 82nd Brig.	
	7		2 Lt. T. REES from Bac.	
	8		1 Off. to Hospital. 1 L.D. Horse killed (shell fire).	
	9		1 Offr. & 1 Lt. Svy. from Bac. 2 L.D. Horse & 1 Mule	
			to Mob. Vet. Sec. 2 Lt. C.H. ATKINSON to 84th Brig.	
	10		2 Lt. O'KEEFE struck off Strength. (4th Army 1-9 A: 11/7/16	
	11		18th Div. Q.P. 37/4 (Further Tactical Instructions) Received	

Army Form C. 2118

WAR DIARY
or
INTELLIGENCE SUMMARY

18th D.A.C.

(Erase heading not required.)

Instructions regarding War Diaries and Intelligence Summaries are contained in F.S. Regs., Part II. and the Staff Manual respectively. Title Pages will be prepared in manuscript.

Place	Date 1916	Hour	Summary of Events and Information	Remarks and references to Appendices
H. 13. Central (France B2=)	July 1st " 13		1 Fitter from Base & Bomb: from 4 & 8 T. Dv. 4 L.D. Horse to 41 L.D. Horse. T.M.S. 6 L.D. Horse to 84 T. Brig. 2 Lt. J.A. INVERARITY to 2/18/T.M. Batty. + 1 Gunner. 18th Div. Q.P. 37/7 re listing of Battle Field Postal + 15 th Div. Q.P. 37/1 re Prisoners of War received. 9 L.D. Horse to 82nd Brig. 1 L.D. Horse each to 84th Brig. + to 5th Brig. 1 Gunner to Base under Age (auth. C.R.5544/432. "A" 27/7/16.) 18th Div. D.P. 37/5 re Medical Arrangements Received. 1 R.1. Horse W.V. Sec "A" Echelon to Bois DES TAILLES.	1 L.D. Horse died.
"	" 14		1 L.D. Horse died. 1 L.D. to 82nd 10 L.D. 84th Brig.	
"	" 15		Officers Changes to 84th Brig.	
"	" 16		2 Lt. to Hospital 1 L.D. Horse died. 1 Horse from Base:- 2 Lts. H.J. CLARKSON-WILLIAMS, P.C. INGLIS, E. ROYSTON-MILLS, E.C.A. DUNCUM, + C.P.T. SHELLEY.	

1875 Wt. W593/826 1,000,000 4/15 J.B.C. & A. A.D.S.S./Forms/C. 2118.

WAR DIARY or INTELLIGENCE SUMMARY

18th D.A. Army Form C. 2118

Place	Date	Hour	Summary of Events and Information	Remarks and references to Appendices
F.14. b/d 1.7 8.4. (Ouma b.3)	6/July/17		H.Q. & "A" Eschelon from BOIS DES TAILLES to SAILLY LAURETTE. T.F.14. b. 8.4. (Br Ouma). 3 hr. & Dr. to 82nd Brig. 6 hr. to 83rd Brig. 9: J/Bomb-85th Brig.	Ey H
	15		3: L.A. & "A" onto A. 84th Brig. 35th Div. Cole (write) Aed. -1 Sergt. & Bomb. 44 hrs. to Dr. from B.me. S.L.D. Horse to M.V. ic. & 85th Brig. -1 Sergt. & Bomb.t & I.L.D. 5 hr. & 15 Dr. - 1 Di. from Hospital.	Sery afair
	4		Brig. to 65th Brig. & 3. L.G. Have to 84th Brig. 1 Multo M.V. ic. Infants. Montend N.R. CRUIKSHANK to 83rd Brig. H.J. CLARKSON-WILLIAMS & 84th Brig. + C.P. LAIT to 84th Brig. + 3 hrs. & 3 Dr. to 84th Brig.	
	20		-5 hr. & 4 Dr. to 83rd Brig. + 5 hr. & 5th Brig. -LIS. F.S. REES & G. ISMAY to 85th Brig. i Corp. S/Smith to Di. Hospital. i Com. S/Smith killed to shell fire.	

Army Form C. 2118

WAR DIARY
or
INTELLIGENCE SUMMARY
(Erase heading not required.)

18th D.A.C.

Place	Date	Hour	Summary of Events and Information	Remarks and references to Appendices
F.19.	4 July 21		6 hr. to 85th Rnj.	
8.9.	" 22		1 Saddler to F H ospital. 1 L.A.H ors to M.V.S.	
(61D)	" 23		Column moved to ARGOEUVES.	
(Somme)	" 24		Column moved to BELLIFONTAINE & BAILLEUL (SOMME)	
ARGOEUVES	" 25		4 S.L.D. +1 Mule from REMOUNTS (ABBEVILLE). 1 Mule to M.V. Sec	
	" 26		18 Dr. from advanced Dpt. ABBEVILLE	
	" 27		1 L.A. Horse left at BAILLEUL. Entrained Pont Remy & Longpré	
	" 28		1 L.A. Horse destroyed M.V.Sec. Arrived at EECKE	
EECKE	" 30		Officer changed to M.V. Sec.	
	" 31		1 L.A. Horse to M.V. Sec.	

[signature] O.C. 18 D.A.C.

Vol 12
Army Form C. 2118

WAR DIARY
or
INTELLIGENCE SUMMARY
(Erase heading not required.)

18th D.A.C.

Place	Date	Hour	Summary of Events and Information	Remarks and references to Appendices
EEKE	Aug 1		3 Dvs. to Hospital. Afternoon I on Training of Drafts from D.A.C. to July. Artillery Brigades have been informed on Results of Recent Inspection.	Appendix I WWI
LE KIRLEM (HAZEBROUCK SA-MAP)	" 3		Column moved to LE KIRLEM on Div. Artillery forming into this — Marched by Sections at 4 from Inthe villers. Route via METÉREN – BAILLEUL. Orders received that D.A.C. was to be emptied of 18 Pr. & 4.5" Ammn. and that its Complement was to be held in forward Schedules.	
	" 4		2 Ammn dvs. discharged from Hospital. Received 184 A.W. "Q" orders (Ammunition Situation) "Instructions on Supply of ammunition" which directed that in future the Supply of Ammunition of all Kinds, including Grenades, Trench Mortar Bombs, Very Lights, Rockets etc will be made through the D.W. Ammn. Col.	
	" 5		5th A.D. N° 1. N°1 + 8 Q Returns to Hospital.	
	" 6		5th A.D. N° 1. N° 1 + 8 Q Received giving Procedure as to Supply of Grenades, Very Lights etc. Supply of Ammn from	

WAR DIARY
or
INTELLIGENCE SUMMARY

(Erase heading not required.)

Army Form C. 2118

18th D.A.C.

Place	Date 1914	Hour	Summary of Events and Information	Remarks and references to Appendices
Le KiRIEM	Aug 6		D.A.C. De-entrained as in Appendix II attached. Bent + Grenade Ship placed under Control of O.C. "B" Echelon and throughout for Supply to Brigade D amm [?] found by A.S.C.	Appendix II Supplts [?] of Ammn at all G.
"	7		Same.	
"	8		1 Drivr from Hospital.	
"	9		1 Drivr to Hospital. 1 O/Rs. to 81st Brig R.F.A. 17th Div.	
"	10		Capt. + 2 Drivrs to Hospital. 20 Gunners & Drivrs from Camp.	
"	11		1 Drivr to Hospital. 2 Drivrs from Hospital.	
"	12		Ammns to Hospital.	
"	13		1 Drivrs civilian to Hospital. 1 Drivr from Hospital	
"	14		2 Drivrs to Hospital. 2 Drivrs from Hospital	
"	15		Sergt. to Hospital. 1 Drivr from Hospital. 53 Gunners	
"	16		10 Drivrs from Base. 10 Gunners + 5 Drivrs to 72nd Bny. R.F.A. " 73rd " 74 " 85	
"	17		19 Gunners + 11 Drivrs from Base. 1 Drivr to Hospital	
"	18		1 Driver to Hospital	

WAR DIARY
or
INTELLIGENCE SUMMARY
(Erase heading not required.)

Army Form C. 2118

18th D.A.C.

Instructions regarding War Diaries and Intelligence Summaries are contained in F.S. Regs., Part II. and the Staff Manual respectively. Title Pages will be prepared in manuscript.

Place	Date	Hour	Summary of Events and Information	Remarks and references to Appendices
LE KURLEN (near STEENWERK)	1915 Aug 19		Weather Cloudy. Heavy Showers.	
	" 20		Cloudy with light Rain. Slight Rain start 1.30 P.M. Training of Drafts :- Telephone Course commenced in D.A.C. 3 bm from F.A. Brigade & 17 bm from D.A.C. form classes of 12 each. Weather Bright. Wind N.E.	
	" 20		Administrative :- Preliminary move orders to Concentration Area received with hand tables & Programme of Reliefs 18th Div. Nos 1,4,12, & A graction of Units Received to Nos 1,2,3,4,5 F.A. Instructions for billetting Parties Recd.	Appendix IV WD 2
			6 L.D. Horse destroyed. 6 L.D. Horses to Mob. Vet. Sec.	
	" 21		Transfers 6 hys & 4 bns to 82nd Brig. R.F.A.	
			4 " 1 " :::	
			5 " 3 & 3	
			2 " 8 & 3	
			2 L.D. Horses to Mob. Vet. Section	
	" 22		Administrative: Instructions Recd. from R.A.H.Q. that Column will	

Army Form C. 2118

WAR DIARY
or
INTELLIGENCE SUMMARY

(Erase heading not required.)

18th D. A. C.

Instructions regarding War Diaries and Intelligence Summaries are contained in F.S. Regs., Part II. and the Staff Manual respectively. Title Pages will be prepared in manuscript.

Place	Date	Hour	Summary of Events and Information	Remarks and references to Appendices
LE HIRLEN	Aug 22		Recd full amm? (1st ANZAC R.A/T/No 86/22.8.16)	
	,, 23		II Instructions received for move of 38th Wagons to Battn? to move into concentration area.	
			III Instructions as to ration for Adv. Party Recd. No SC 554	
			IV " " Dumped Boxed Amm? "	
			V Returning orders recd.	
			Weather Cloudy with light breeze.	
			Lt G.E. MILLS & N.C.O's Instructing Party sent to new area.	
			36 Mules & 4 R. Horses from Remounts.	
			1 B.S.M. & Bo. & 3 Drivers from Base.	
			Weather Bright with first frost.	
	,, 24		Weather cloudy with bright sun.	
	,, 25		1 Sgt. to H of Field.	
	,, 26		1 L.D. Horse died. Weather:- Some rain during [?]noon, intermittent sunshine bright in afternoon with strong breeze.	
	,, 27		All Batteries filled from 3rd D.A.C. Instructions received from H.Q. R.A. 18th Div. to send round	

1875. Wt. W593/826. 1,000,000 4/15 J.B.C. & A. A.D.S.S./Forms/C. 2118.

Army Form C. 2118

WAR DIARY
or
INTELLIGENCE SUMMARY
(Erase heading not required.)

Place	Date	Hour	Summary of Events and Information	Remarks and references to Appendices
LE RIRLEM	Aug 27		Ammunition to BAILLEUL Station. So to clear S.S. Wagons to move extra Baggage. Weather: dull & Calm	
	28		Column commenced entraining at BAILLEUL in accordance with instructions received from H.Q. R.A. 18 Div. Weather:- Dull, Snow showers	
AUTHUILE	29		16 guns from Bde. Entraining at BAILLEUL continued. H.Q. & Column arrived at DOULLENS @ 4.15 P.M. Column concentrated at AUTHUILE instructions received for move to VAL DE MAISON on 30.8.18. Weather:- Cloudy with strong wind & heavy rain showers.	
VAL DE MAISON	30		Column moved to VAL DE MAISON at 1-30 morning at destination @ 4-30 P.M. Artillery Operation Orders. Weather:- Cloudy, strong wind & heavy rain.	
	31		No. 8 received. No. 3 Section to move to HEADAUVILLE Orders received from O.C. 25 Bde. D.A.C. & report to	

Appendix I

Memorandum on
The training of personnel of a D.A.C. with a view to replacing Casualties in Field Artillery Brigades during Stationary Warfare.

----

1. **DRIVERS.** The normal instructions and duties in a Divisional Ammunition Column are appropriate and sufficient for training purposes and drafts sent to batteries should be adequately trained to take their places in teams immediately on arrival.

2. **GUNNERS.** The training of Gunners in a Divisional Ammunition Column is a question worthy of consideration. During the operations North of the Somme between June 28th and July 21/1916 the 18th Divisional Ammunition Column, tranferred to the four Artillery Brigades of the Division, about 80 Gunners to replace casualties. No instructions in gun drill was, or could have been given to these Gunners while they were in the Ammunition Column, because no means of imparting practical knowledge were available.

   It is obvious that the actual value of these drafts - arriving as they did at a period of high pressure - would have been sensibly increased by training in the Ammunition Column, during the period of low pressure immediately preceding the entry of the Division into the Line. Such a course of training as is here suggested could be carried out if the requisite personnel and material were available. The provision of a Gun with Sights and Instruments - whether real or dummy - is of course essential. In addition a small instructional staff should be kept with the Column for special training work. If the Officer Commanding the Ammunition Column were provided these facilities he should then be able to increase materially the fighting value of the Gunners sent with drafts to the Field Artillery Brigades, and, what to all intents and purposes would constitute a Mobile Artillery Training Centre would be formed within the Division.

   Other features might be added as the result of experience.

Appendix II

CHANNELS OF AMMUNITION SUPPLY (OUTWARDS) FROM
18th Divisional Amm. Col.

Nature of Ammn.	From.	To.
A. Ax. B.Bx. Pistol & S.A.A.	No 1 Section D.A.C.	8th R. Sussex Pioneers 82nd Brigade R.F.A. A/85th and 53rd Inf. Brigade.
A. Ax. B.Bx. Pistol & S.A.A.	No 2 Section D.A.C.	83rd Brigade R.F.A. B/85th and 54th Inf. Brigade.
A. Ax. B.Bx. Pistol & S.A.A.	No 3 Section D.A.C.	84th Brigade R.F.A. C/85th and 55th Inf. Brigade.
Grenades, Lights, Rockets, Cartridges, Cups, Candles, etc.	No 4 Section D.A.C.	All Inf. Bde. Bomb Stores.

Lieut Col. R.F.A.
Commanding 18th Div. Amm. Column.

12.8.16.

S E C R E T.

18th/Div/No/49/22   (A)

The following will be the location of Units of 18th Division in the new Area, reference Map Sheets 36 B. and 51 c. $\frac{1}{40,000}$.

Divisional Troops Group (to be billeted by Staff Officer 18th Division.)

18th Divisional Headquarters.)	
A.D.M.S. ")	
A.D.V.S. ")	
D.A.D.O.S. ")	ROELLECOURT.
S.O.F. ")	
Headquarters, Divisional Train)	
Headquarters, R.E.	BOIRIN.
8th R.Sussex Pioneers.	LE QUESNEL.
56th Field Ambulance	L'ABBAYE de NEUVILLE Fme.
150th Company, Train	ROCOURT ST LAURENT.
30th Mobile Vet.Section.	LE QUESNEL
35th Sanitary Section	ROELLECOURT.

Artillery Group (to be billeted by Staff Officer R.A.)

Headquarters, Divisional R.A.	ST MICHEL-SUR-TERNOISE.
82nd Brigade R.F.A.)	
83rd Brigade R.F.A.)	
84th Brigade R.F.A.)	Vicinity of
85th Brigade R.F.A.)	ST MICHEL-SUR-TERNOISE.
18th D.A.C.)	
Medium Trench Mortar Battys.)	

53rd Brigade Group (to be billeted by Staff Officer 53rd Infantry Brigade)

53rd Brigade Headquarters.	CHELERS.
1 Battalion	"
1 Battalion	GUESTREVILLE.
1 Battalion	BETHONSART.
1 Battalion	VILLERS BRULIN.
53rd Machine Gun Company	"
53rd Trench Mortar Battery	BETHONSART.
79th Field Co. R.E.	BETHENCOURT.
151st Company, Train.	TINQUES.

P.T.O.

54th Brigade Group (to be billeted by Staff Officer 54th
                    Infantry Brigade)

54th Brigade Headquarters   LE THIEULOYE.

2 Battalions   "
1 Battalion   MARQUAY.
1 Battalion   ORLENCOURT
54th Machine Gun Company   "
54th Trench Mortar Battery

80th Field Co. R.E.   BAILLEUL-AUX-CORNAILLES.

54th Field Ambulance   "

152nd Company Train   "

55th Brigade Group (to be billeted by Staff Officer 55th Infantry
                    Brigade)

55th Brigade Headquarters.   MONCHY-BRETON.

2 Battalions   "

2 Battalions   MAGNICOURT-EN-COMTE.

55th Machine Gun Company   ROCOURT.

55th Trench Mortar Battery   MONCHY-BRETON.

92nd Field Co. R.E.   MAGNICOURT-EN-COMTE.

55th Field Ambulance   TINCQUETTE.

153rd Company Train   TINQUES.

                                                    Captain,
                                      D.A.A. & Q.M.G., 18th Division.

20th August 1916.

Copies to:-
   'G'   53rd Inf. Bde.
   D.A.D.O.S.   54th Inf. Bde.
   A.P.M.   55th   "   "
   S.O.F.   8th R. Sussex Pioneers.
   A.D.V.S.   18th Div. Train.
   18th Div. Art.   O.C., R.A.M.C.
   R.E.

War Diary

18th D.A.C.

Army Form C. 2118
Vol 3
18th D.A-C.

WAR DIARY
or
INTELLIGENCE SUMMARY
(Erase heading not required.)

Instructions regarding War Diaries and Intelligence Summaries are contained in F.S. Regs., Part II. and the Staff Manual respectively. Title Pages will be prepared in manuscript.

Place	Date	Hour	Summary of Events and Information	Remarks and references to Appendices
VAL DE MAISON	Sept 1		Weather:- Bright at times, slight showers, some rain. 1 D. to Hospital. 1 Sergt. from B we. Notification received that Column will move to some other Area. 18th D.V. R.A. Column orders received which include details for move of Column to BRICKFIELDS Area, ALBERT. Weather:- Calm, dry, + fair amount of sunshine	
ALBERT	3		Head of Column arrived at 1 M.U. from ALBERT on BOUZINCOURT Rd. at 10-30 A.M. and camped on North side of Road. R.A. formation with N.U. is Head. Weather:- Fine in morning. Showers during afternoon. 1 mule lost.	
"	4		1 L.A. Horse to M.of.Vet. Section. Weather:- Cloudy, rain during afternoon + night.	
"	5		Weather:- Cloudy, some rain.	
"	6		1 L.A. Horse to M.of.Vet. Section. Barometer 29.75 at 1 P.M.	
"	7		Weather:- A mild to clear day. Barometer 30.00 @ 9 A.M. 1 B.S.M. to 82nd Bng. 1 D. to Hospital. Weather:-	
"	8		Fine fair amount of Sunshine. Barometer 30.1 @ 9 A.M. 1 Mule killed by shell fire. 1 L.A. Horse to M. of. Vet. Section. Weather:- Cloudy, dry. Barometer 30.075 @ 9 A.M. 3 Sectns Informed Column	

Army Form C. 2118

WAR DIARY
or
INTELLIGENCE SUMMARY
(Erase heading not required.)

18th – D.A.C.

Instructions regarding War Diaries and Intelligence Summaries are contained in F.S. Regs., Part II. and the Staff Manual respectively. Title Pages will be prepared in manuscript.

Place	Date 1916	Hour	Summary of Events and Information	Remarks and references to Appendices
ALBERT	Sept 9		9 L.D. Horses to Mob. Vet. Section. Weather:- Dry/Sunshine & light Breeze. Barometer 30.05 @ 9 A.M.	
"	10		1 R. & L.D. Horse to Mob. Vet. Section. Weather:- Stock Old wind in morning. Sunshine d to 5 P.M. Barometer 29.975 @ 9 A.M.	
			1 D. to Hospital. Posting to Brigades:-	
			4 Gun & 7 Am. to 82nd Brig	
			2 " " " 83 "	
			2 " " " 84 "	
			2 " " " 85 "	
			The following officers posted attached to Brigade for Instruction:- 2/Lt THORP & 2/Lt PRENDERGAST to 83 Brig. 2/Lt INGLIS & 2/Lt DUNCUM to 84 Brig. 2/Lt E.J. PEARSON & 2/Lt ROBOTTOM to 85 Brig. 2/Lt NICHOLS attached to 82nd Brig.	
"	11		Weather:- Dry & light, Barometer 29.93 @ 9 A.M. Cold morning & night, afternoon cloudy. No Instructions.	
"	12		1 Horse & 1 Mule to Mob. Vet. Section. Barometer 29.90 @ 9 A.M. Dull & Showery	
"	13		1 L.D. Horse & 1 Mule to Mob. Vet. Section. Dull & Showery. 1 Driver from Base	

WAR DIARY
or
INTELLIGENCE SUMMARY   18th D.A.C.

Army Form C. 2118

Place	Date 1916	Hour	Summary of Events and Information	Remarks and references to Appendices
ALBERT	Sept 14	9 A.M.	Weather:- Cloudy, wind, some rain. Barometer :- 29.93 9 A.M. 2 Men + 1 5th to Hospital. A demonstration :- following received (1) 18" Div: S.W. 1.8.18.41. "First of two pigeons" (2) 18" Div: 9/R/5 "Cleaning a Battlefield" (3) 18" Div: 8.1. 9/R/16 Instructions to hostile aircraft. (4) 18" Div: 834 "Rifle & machine gun fire on aircraft".	
	- 15		Weather:- Morning bright, afternoon dull. Cold. Barometer 30.025 9 A.M. 1 Man to Hospital. 2 L.D. Horses to Mob. Vet. Section	
	- 16		Weather:- Dull + cold. Barometer 29.93 9 A.M. A demonstration. 10 L.D. Horses to Mob. Vet. & other. Column to move to V.30.a. 18 R.A. Sec. 100 received Sheet ALBERT 1/40,000. Column moved W 25 at 6. month to Home. Weather:- Bright, fresh wind.	
	- 17		Barometer 30.10 @ 9 A.M.	
	- 18		1 Gr. to Hospital. Weather:- Heavy rain all day. Barometer 2 9.15 falling @ 9 A.M.	
	- 19		13 E.D. Horses from B[?] 22 O.R. from Bar. Weather:- Heavy Storm. Rain at intervals all day. Barometer 29.31 @ 9 A.M.	

WAR DIARY
or
INTELLIGENCE SUMMARY

Army Form C. 2118

13th D.A.C.

Place	Date	Hour	Summary of Events and Information	Remarks and references to Appendices
ALBERT AREA.	Sept 20		1 Sgt. to Hospital. Weather:- Fine all day. Bomb't at night. Barom'r 29.5 @ 9 A.M.	
	" 21		8. L.D. Horse to Mob. Vet. Section. Weather:- Rain at intervals. Barom'r 30.00 @ 9 A.M.	
	" 22		H.Q. D.A.C. moved to W. 25. a. o.b. ALBERT. Shot 1/40:00 at 2:45 P.M. — Dr. to Base. Weather:- truth- munitions & other returns. Brim. Barom'r 29.7 at 9 A.M. Fine + bright.	
	" 23		Weather:- Fine much sunshine - Barom'r 29.50 @ 9 A.M.	
	" 24		2 warning officers arrived:- Capt: A.E. BUDDEN, J/H T.N. BERRY, J/H N HOTTON H.A.S. ROBINSON 1/H J. DONELLY & J/H WILLIAMS (all R.F.A.) Weather:- Heavy fog up to midday, afternoon bright sunshine. Barom'r 29.75 @ 9 A.M.	
	" 25		Lt Col. 2/C Johnston, own C.O. Inspection parade	
	26.		1st Col M.B. Jobb. — left 12 DAC for England. 2nd weather from Comy RHC — 2nd Col Z.C. Johnston R.F.A. took over command of 13th DAC.	

WAR DIARY
or
INTELLIGENCE SUMMARY
(Erase heading not required.)

Army Form C. 2118

Place	Date	Hour	Summary of Events and Information	Remarks and references to Appendices
Albert Area.	27	—	Horses evacuated to M.V.S. from — No 2 Section — 9 L.D. & Bucks. weather fine. Strong breeze.	
"	28	—	Horses evacuated to M.V.S. from No II Section 9 L.D. & 14 D. Strayed (seven) horses Cochran plyls.) Arrived from Rd Chief 2 R & 19 L.D. These to join his gun reserves to this sent for batteries of 18" Div.	
"	29	—	F.G.C.M. on Driver Marshall "I" section. Pres. Lieut Capt. J. O'Neil. Rav.son this evening 999g. Herns No 7 Schn — I.L.D.T. M.V.S. Sent to order No 19. Section 1 A.D.A.C. To remain Platoon. eng. at present.	
"	30	—	Valuthum from [?] Bouge. Orders from 18th Div. A.M.S/um. R.E.M. Patrick 32 wagons to Avelure	

F. E. Johnston
Lt. Col.
Comdg 18th Div. Ammn Column.

18th DIVISIONAL ARTILLERY ORDER No.9.

by Brig.General S.F.Metcalfe, D.S.O.

1. The relief of 2nd Australian Divisional Artillery by 18th Div. Art. will be carried out on 3rd September in accordance with the following instructions.

2. The 85th Brigade R.F.A. will relieve the 22nd Australian Brigade by sections, first section at 12 noon, second section at 4.0 p.m. Registration will be carried out during the day. 85th Brigade R.F.A. will assume responsibility for the defence of 22nd Australian Brigade front at 4.0 p.m.

3. The 83rd Brigade R.F.A. will remain in present positions and will be responsible for defence of front covered by 4th Australian Brigade R.F.A. from 12 noon. Any necessary registration will be carried out before that hour.

4. The 82nd Brigade R.F.A. will rejoin 18th Divisional Artillery but will remain in present positions and will assume responsibility for defence of front covered by 6th Australian Brigade from 12 noon. All necessary registration being carried out previous to that hour.

5. The 84th Brigade R.F.A. will rejoin 18th Divisional Artillery at 12 noon on 3rd September and will relieve 5th Australian Brigade by sections, first section at 12 noon, 2nd section at 4 p.m.
The 84th Brigade R.F.A. will assume responsibility for 5th Australian Brigade front from 4 p.m.

6. 82nd, 83rd, 84th & 85th Brigade Commanders will communicate with the respective 2nd Australian Div.Art. Brigade Commanders whom they are about to relieve, with a view to obtaining all possible information concerning the fronts they are about to cover.

7. The 18th D.A.C. will relieve 2nd Australian D.A.C. on the 3rd Sept. and will assume responsibility for supply of ammunition from 12 noon. The 18th D.A.C. will march from VAL DE MAISON, head of the Column to start at 5 a.m., column to march in 5 sections, 300 yards between sections. Route:- HERISSART - CONTAY - SENLIS - BOUZINCOURT. Advanced details for quartering to report to Commandant, BRICKFIELDS area, ½ mile N.W. of ALBERT on ALBERT - BOUZINCOURT road.

8. No.3 Section D.A.C. at present attached to 25th D.A.C. will rejoin 18th D.A.C. in new billets (BRICKFIELDS area) on the 3rd marching at 2 p.m. via BOUZINCOURT.

9. H.Q.18th Divisional Artillery will assume responsibility for defence of the line from 5 p.m. on September 3rd.

10. 18th Divisional Artillery Report Centre will close at RUBEMPRE at 10.0 a.m. on 3rd inst., and reopen at TARA Redoubt 1½ miles N.E. of ALBERT on ALBERT-BAPAUME Road.

11. All surplus ammunition held by 22nd and 5th Australian Brigades will be taken over by 85th and 84th Brigades respectively in the gun pits.

P.T.O.

-2-

12. Please acknowledge.

[signature]

Captain R.A.,
Brigade Major R.A., 18th Division.

2/9/16.

Copies to:-
    1st Anzac.
    2nd Australian Div.Art.
    LAHORE Div.Art.
    25th Div.Art.
    82nd Brigade R.F.A.
    83rd   "   " "
    84th   "   " "
    85th
    D.A.C. (1 copy for No.3 Section).
    Commandant (BRICKFIELDS.
    18th Division.
    4th Australian Div.Art.
    150th Coy. A.S.C.

App. Ia B176

AMENDMENTS to 18th Divisional Artillery Operation Order No.9.

In accordance with instructions received from 1st ANZAC R.A. 18th Div.Art. Order No.9 is amended as under:-

Para 2.
The relief of 22nd Australian Brigade R.F.A. by 85th Brigade R.F.A. is amended as under:-

First Section per battery 12 noon Sept.3rd.
Second   "   "   "   12 noon   " 4th.
Bde H.Q.   12 noon   " 4th.

Para. 5.
The relief of 5th Australian Brigade R.F.A. by 84th Bde.R.F.A. is amended as under:-

The 84th Bde.R.F.A.(less one section per battery) will remain under orders of 25th Divn. until 12 noon on Sept. 4th.
One section per battery of 84th Bde. will relieve one section per battery 5th Australian Brigade at 12 noon on Sept.3rd.
Remaining sections and Bde. H.Q. at 12 noon on Sept.4th.

Para. 8.
No.3 Section D.A.C. will rejoin 18th D.A.C. on 4th instead of 5th instant.

A.T.Brooke
Captain R.A.,
Brigade Major R.A.,18th Division.

H.Q.R.A.,18th Divn.
2nd Sept. 1916.

Copies to all concerned.

18th. Divisional Artillery. No. 10.

by Brig. Gen. S.F. Metcalfe, D.S.O.

Copy No. 24.

1. The relief of 2nd Australian Divisional Artillery by 18th Divisional Artillery will be completed to-morrow September 4th. as under:-

2. 82nd. Brigade R.F.A.

   The 82nd. Brigade will come under control of 18th. Div. Art. from 6-0pm on 4th.
   All necessary preparations will be made to take over responsibility for defence of front covered by 6th Australian Brigade by 2pm at which hour the latter Brigade will be withdrawn from the line.

3. 83rd. Brigade R.F.A.

   The 83rd. Brigade R.F.A. will be responsible for front at present covered by 4th Xxxixxixxx Brigade R.F.A. from 10am at which time the latter Brigade will be withdrawn.

4. 84th. Brigade R.F.A.

   The 84th Brigade R.F.A. will rejoin 18th. Divisional Artillery from 5am on Sept. 4th and will relieve 5th Australian Brigade as under:-
   1st Sections at 6am. 2nd Sections and Brigade H.Q. at 12 noon.

5. 85th. Brigade R.F.A.

   The 85th Brigade R.F.A. will relieve 22nd. Australian Brigade R.F.A. on Sept. 4th as under:-
   Remaining section and Brigade H.Q. at 10am.

6. Divisional Artillery H.Q.

   18th. Div. Art. H.Q. will relieve 2nd. Australian Div. Art H.Q. at 10am on Sept.4th

7. Previous to relieve Brigades will acquaint THEMSELVES with existing system of Liaison Officers provided with the Infantry and ascertain the exact positions of Brigade and Battalion H.Q. supported by their Brigades.

8. Wireless masts are allotted as follows:-
   one mast at present shared by 5th and 6th Australian Bdes. will be taken over by 84th Bde. and will be shared by 82nd and 84th Bdes. One mast at present with 4th Australian Bde will be taken over by 83rd Bde and will be shared by 85th and 83rd Bdes.

9. All moves of D.A.C. remain as ordered in Artillery Order No. 9.

10. Please acknowledge.

Sd. A.T. Brooke Capt. R.A.
Brigade Major R.A. 18th. Division.

SECRET.

Subject:- Clearing the Battlefield.

18th Division C.R.S.

The clearing of the battlefield resolves itself into three main tasks :-

1. The removal of the wounded, under arrangements made by the Medical Authorities.

2. The burial of the dead.

3. The salvage of all battle material and stores, whether useful or otherwise.

With reference to (2) :-

(a). Responsibility.

A battalion is primarily responsible for the burial of its own dead, as soon as possible after death.

When the Division takes over a line which is already cumbered with dead, all Units, without waiting for orders, must set to work to bury the dead in their own areas and in the vicinity of their trenches.

If battalions are unable to cope with the work, they must apply to the Brigade for assistance.

Brigades, if they require further assistance, must notify the D.H.Q., and state the place where burial parties are needed.

The insanitary practice of leaving corpses lying about in, or in the vicinity of, trenches, for someone else to bury is not to be tolerated.

Commanding Officers and Company Commanders must take the necessary steps without waiting for orders.

(b) Method.

As far as possible bodies should be collected and

2.

buried in a few selected spots, and not scattered about
in individual graves.

The Officer or Chaplain in charge of burial party
will personally see that each body is searched before
interment, and will make a note of the name and number of each
body from the identity disc, and also of the location of the
grave. These notes should be forwarded to the Adjutant of
the unit or the Staff Captain concerned. All effects of each
man to be tied together with the cord of his identity disc,
and sent to the Adjutant of his unit.

Each grave should be marked in some way so as to assist
subsequent identifications. Pegs with labels can be obtained
from the Graves Registration units for this purpose.

The important point is to get the dead buried as soon as
possible, but it is hardly necessary to emphasize the fact
that all possible care should be taken, for the sake of
relatives and friends at home, to mark the graves so that
they can be easily identified afterwards.

With reference to (3) :-

Spots for salvage dumps must be selected by battalions,
Brigades and Division, and should be situated as near as
possible to the route followed by the wagons bringing up
the daily rations.

Battalions are responsible for collecting every sort
of debris and war material, littering the ground occupied by
them, into their battalion salvage dump.

Brigades will be responsible for clearing these
battalion dumps into the Brigade dump.

The Division is responsible for the clearing of
Brigade dumps into the Divisional dump, and for the sorting
and subsequent evacuation of all materials to the departments
concerned.

This salvage work should commence from the moment the

3.

Division takes over a bit of the line, and continue daily as long as there is any material to be removed. Returning ration wagons will be utilized for clearing advanced dumps, Battalion or Brigade, direct to Divisional dump.

As long as there are stores to be removed from these dumps, a ration wagon should never return empty.

Whenever circumstances permit, battalions should detail regimental police to patrol the battlefield, with orders to prevent the looting of the dead, and to prevent unauthorized people from wandering about the battlefield in search of souvenirs.

E. V. Riddell.
Lt. Colonel.
14th Sept.1916.   A.A. & Q.M.G. 18th Division.

App IV

18th Div. No. Q.R. 6.

Subject. Instructions in the event of an
Advance.

SECRET

1. All Units are to be prepared to move at 6 hours notice and to march with the Baggage and Stores laid down in G 1098, and such authorised stores as have been authorised in G.R.Os.

2. Baggage wagons will at once rejoin Units and will remain with them They are to be kept loaded as far as possible and arrangements are to be made to complete their loading at short notice.

3. All surplus baggage and stores which cannot be carried are to be dumped. Brigades will arrange with Town Majors for suitable Buildings to be allotted for the storage of surplus baggage and stores of Brigade groups.
    Men to be left in charge are to be detailed and their numbers to be reported to this Office. Three days preserved rations are to be left with these parties.

4.. All surplus Ordnance stores which cannot be carried are to be returned to D.A.D.O.S. They are not to be dumped as was done at PICQUIGNY in May.

sd E.V. Riddell Lieut Col.
A.A. Q.M.G. 18th Division.

18th September 1916.

SECRET.

O.C.
18th. D.A.C.

S.S. 100.

App. V

Will you please arrange to move your column from the site which you now occupy to one immediately north of road which passes through square V.30.b.W.25 A. and B.   Reference map. Albert 1/40,000.

Your area will be within the 500 yards squares above mentioned.   The move should be made at once if possible to-day.   Will you please report to this office and also to the Camp Commandant, Brickfields when the move is completed and also please forward the exact locations as soon as they have been determined of your four Sections and Headquarters.

           Sd. E. Edwards, Capt, R.A.
         Staff Capt. R.A. 18th. Division.

17.9.16.

Vol 14

War Diary
for
October 1916

18th Div. Amm. Col.

WAR DIARY or INTELLIGENCE SUMMARY

Army Form C. 2118

(Erase heading not required.)

Instructions regarding War Diaries and Intelligence Summaries are contained in F. S. Regs., Part II. and the Staff Manual respectively. Title Pages will be prepared in manuscript.

18th DIVISION
AMMUNITION C[OLUMN]
No. [illegible]

Place	Date	Hour	Summary of Events and Information	Remarks and references to Appendices
Albert	Oct 1	.	1 Driver to Hospital.	
	" 2	.	1 Driver evacuated sick. 1 Driver to Hospital.	
	" 3	.	3 L.D. Horses to M.V.S. 1 Driver to Hospital.	
	" 4	.	1 Gunner to Hospital.	
	" 5	.	1 Driver evacuated sick.	
	" 6	.	2 Gunners & 2 Drivers to Hospital. 1 Mule to M.V.S.	
	" 7	.	4 Gunners & 1 Bombardier to 82 Brigade. 4 Gunners to 83 Bty. 16	
	" 8	.	4 Gunners & 2 Bombardiers to 84 Brigade. 1 Gunner & 1 Bombr.	
	" 9	.	4 Gunners to 85 Brigade.	
	" 10	.	1 Driver evacuated from Hospital. 1 L.D. Horse to M.V.S.	
	" 11	.	1 L.D. Horse to M.V.S.	
	" 12	.	Postings from 302 Base Depot: 7 Gunners, 13 Drivers & 1 Bombardier for D. Battery, 82 Brigade.	
	" 13	.	Postings from No 2 Base Depot: 4 Gunners 58.	
	" 14	.	2 Drivers to Hospital. 7 Horses to [?]	
	" 15	.	2 [?] 75 Horses to [?] Sick.	

WAR DIARY or INTELLIGENCE SUMMARY

Army Form C. 2118

18th DIVISION
AMMUNITION COL[UMN]

Place	Date	Hour	Summary of Events and Information	Remarks and references to Appendices
Albert. Delto.	16th		1 Gunner & 2 Drivers evacuated Sick.	
	17th		Capt. from J.T.O'Neill Power No.4 Section ordered to England for duty. 2nd Lieut. Dorothy hastened to Y.T.M. Battery. 2 Drivers to Hospital & 1 Gunner & 1 Driver evacuated.	
	18th		Transfers 7 to 82nd Brigade, 7 Gunners & 9 Drivers, 7 to 83rd Brigade, 12 Gunners & 2 Drivers, 7 to 84th Brigade 5 Gunners & 9 Drivers, 7 to 85th Brigade 8 Gunners & 6 Drivers, 7 to Y.M. Battery 8 Gunners.	
	19th		Capt. James R.A.M.C. arrived from 55th Field Ambulance. Lieut. T. Gates R.A.M.C. left to join the above unit. Postings from the 39th Base 8 Gunners - Driver 8/n Batt. 9 Gunners. No 2 Base 1 B.S.M. 1 Corpl. and 1 Bomb on Driver 2 Gunners.	
	20th		Postings from 39th Base, 23 Gunners, 17 Drivers 8 I.Q.M.S. 7 Pte. 1 Sgt. sent to Hospital.	
	22nd		1 Driver to Hospital 1 Gunner & 1 Driver evacuated sick	
	24th		1 Driver to Hospital.	
	26th		1 Gunner & 1 Driver to Hospital 1 B.S.M. 1 Driver to M.V.S.	

Army Form C. 2118

18th D... ...AL
AMMUNITI... ...MN.
No. ...

WAR DIARY
or
INTELLIGENCE SUMMARY

(Erase heading not required.)

Instructions regarding War Diaries and Intelligence Summaries are contained in F. S. Regs., Part II. and the Staff Manual respectively. Title Pages will be prepared in manuscript.

Place	Date	Hour	Summary of Events and Information	Remarks and references to Appendices
Albert	Dec 27th		1 Driver to Hospital, Lieut Lawrence No 1 Section Invalidened to 85th Brigade.	
	28th		1 Sr Jasper to Hospital.	
	30th		Lieut Tytler 83rd Brigade just returned 18th DAC. to take over No 1 Section vice Captain Power.	
	31st		1 Gunner Driver to Hospital.	

F. E. Johnston
Lieut. Colonel, R.F.A.
Com'g 18th Div. Ammⁿ Column.

War Diary
for
November 1916

18th D.A.C.

WAR DIARY
or
INTELLIGENCE SUMMARY

(Erase heading not required.)

Army Form C. 2118
10th DIVISIONAL AMMUNITION COLUMN.
No. ....

Instructions regarding War Diaries and Intelligence Summaries are contained in F.S. Regs., Part II. and the Staff Manual respectively. Title Pages will be prepared in manuscript.

Place	Date	Hour	Summary of Events and Information	Remarks and references to Appendices
ALBERT	Nov 1st	—	One Driver to Hospital. "Evacuated." Postings:- 1 Btr; 1 S. Smith to 82nd Bde; 1 Farrier Sgt to 84 Bde; 1 Fitter 8 MS to 85 Bde.	
	2nd	—	Posting:- From R.H. & R.F.A. Base to D.A.C. 2 Corpl; 2 Btrs 1.8 MS	
		—	" " " " " — 50th " — " " 2 Sergts.	
	3rd	—	Postings From R.H. & R.F.A. Base to DAC 2 Sgts; 9 Grs; 1 Dr.	
	"	—	" " 48th " — " " — " 2 Grs.	
	"	—	" " to 83 Bde 1 Bomb.	
	"	—	DAC to Hospital.	
	"	—	One Driver admitted to Hospital.	
	4th	—	Postings: DAC to 82nd Bde - 1 Sgt; 6 Grs; 5 Drs.	
	"	—	" DAC to 84 " -1-; 4 "; 5 "	
	"	—	" DAC to 65th " -1-; 1 Corpl, 1 Bt; 1 Sgt; 1 Dr.	
	5th	—	Hospital. 2 Drivers admitted.	
	"	—	Horses:- 1. L.B.M. Shot; 7 L.D.H. 1 R.H. & 2. Mls to M.V.S.	
	6th	—	Postings: DAC to 82nd Bde. 1 Driver. Hospital:- One Saddler admitted. 1 Driver discharged.	
	8th	—	Postings:- 49 Base to DAC. 1 Farr Sgt. 1 Saddler. 1 S. Smith	
	"	—	Horses:- 1 M. 1 L.D to M.V.S.	
	9th	—	Officers:- 2/Lt E.L. Clarke; 2/Lt L.B. Gardiner joined.	
	"	—	Horses:- 7 L.D to M.V.S.	
	10th	—	Officers:- 2/Lt F.H. McCombie joined.	

WAR DIARY
or
INTELLIGENCE SUMMARY
(Erase heading not required.)

Army Form C. 2118
H.Q. 1st DIVISIONAL AMMUNITION COLUMN.

Place	Date	Hour	Summary of Events and Information	Remarks and references to Appendices
ALBERT	10th	—	Postings:- R.H.R.F.A. Base to D.A.C. 4 Gunners 7. Drivers.	
	11th	—	Postings:- R.H.R.F.A. Base to 50th Base to — 25 Drs.	
		—	Horses:- 2. R. to M.V.S. — 10 Grs. 1 Dr.	
	13th	—	Horses:- 3 L.D. and 1 M. to M.V.S.	
	14th	—	Horses:- 2 L.D. to M.V.S.	
	15th	—	Officers:- Captain W.S. Webster to No 12. A.A. Br. for instruction	
	16th	—	Horses:- 1 L.D. to M.V.S.	
		—	Postings:- R.H.R.F.A. Base to D.A.C. 2 Grs 2 Drs. 1 Sgt. 1 Sr admitted	
	17th	—	to Hospital. 2 Lt Stirling to Hospital.	
		—	Officers:- R.H.R.F.A. Base to D.A.C. 2 Brs from 50th Base 1 Dr.	
		—	Postings:- from 46 D.A.C. Base 1 Dr. D.A.C. to 83 Bde 1 aBr. 1 Farr Sgt. 1 Drk	
		—	to 84 Bde 2 Corpl. D.A.C. to 85 2 Sgt. 1 Saddler.	
	18th	—	Horses:- 1 M. to M.V.S., 1 Br to Y. Br. T.M. 1 Dr. from	
		—	Hospital. 1 Br discharged. 2 Lt Donnelly to 5th Army T.M. School	
		—	Y. Br. T.M. to 2 Lt H.C.L. 2 Lt Skelly 1 M.V.S.	
	19th	—	Officers:- 8. L.D. and 1 M.V.S.	
	20th	—	Horses:- 1 M. to M.V.S. Falke, attached to 9. # A Br for instruction	
	21/3st	—	Officers:- major W.T. Falke, attached to 9. # A Br for instruction	
	23rd	—	to England. major R.H.R.F.A. Base 12 Grs. 21. Drs. 4 L.B. M.V.S.	
	24th	—	Postings:- from R.H.R.F.A. Base 12 Grs. 21. Drs. 4 L.B. Gunnery Course	
	25th	—	Posting:- 4 Brs to 83 Bde 2 Lieut Gardiner to Gunnery Course 5th Army School.	

WAR DIARY
or
INTELLIGENCE SUMMARY

(Erase heading not required.)

Army Form C. 2118

Place	Date	Hour	Summary of Events and Information	Remarks and references to Appendices
ALBERT	26th	—	1 Bt. to Hospital	
	28	—	Posting. 1 Sgt 2 Cpls 4 Bmbrs 14 Grs from W/118 T.M. By.	
	"	—	1 Sgt 1 R. Hospital. Secret move orders recd.	
	29th	—	Horses, 3 R. 24 L.D.M. from Base. Move orders Cancelled.	
	30th	—	Notification recd that 5 Offrs 65 O.R. 86 horses will join Bac from Batteries, on re-organization. Move orders recd stating Bac will move on the 4th Dec 1916. Wagon details exfor Batteries for the move.	

Field
30-11-16

J. E. Johnston
Lt Colonel R.F.A.
O.C. 18. D.A.C.

Vol 116

Confidential
War Diary of
18th Divisional Ammunition Column, C.E.F.
From December 1st 1916 to December 31st 1916.
(Volume VI)

Army Form C. 2118

WAR DIARY
or
INTELLIGENCE SUMMARY
(Erase heading not required.)

Instructions regarding War Diaries and Intelligence Summaries are contained in F.S. Regs., Part II. and the Staff Manual respectively. Title Pages will be prepared in manuscript.

Place	Date	Hour	Summary of Events and Information	Remarks and references to Appendices
ALBERT	1st	—	Horses. 1. L.D. 1 Mule. to M.V.S.	
	2nd	—	— " — 8 Mules received from Base.	
	3rd	—	Sergt Gilbert returned to duty from Hospital. 1 Horse. to M.V.S. Personnel – Officers 2.6, O.R. 61 Hyères, details joined from 95 Bde.	
	4th		Hospital. 1 Driver	
	5th		Officers – 2Lt McCombie, 2Lt Williams, sent in T.M. Course	
	6th		H.Q. 2d 18 Inc. No. 3 Sec arrived at L.H. FR.E. for Training re. No. 1 Sec at N of GLAVIERS. No. 2 Sec. at St Nicolas. No. 4. CAOURS. Hospital. one O.R. admitted.	
LHEVRE	7th		Officers. Lt Donnelly posted to Y. 115 T.M.B. Lt Genny from 83 Bde Horse. + 2 O.S. to M.V.S.	
	8th		to 18 D.A.C.	
	9th		Reinforcements from Base. 19 Drs 12 Grs	
	10th		Hospital 1 Capt. 1 Dr. Signalling Course, 8 men sent to R.E.	
	11th		Officers – 2Lt Clark, evacuated sick.	
	12th		Hospital 1 Capt. 1 L.D. Cork. 2 L.D. Left with Town major ungit 12. L.D. to M.V.S. 1. L.D. destroyed to travel. 9. O.R.	
	13th		Reinforcements from Base.	
	14th		Hospital. 1 Driver.	
	15th		from Base. 14. O.R. 9 Lee to Base (under age) 1. 2. Dro to Hospital	

Army Form C. 2118

WAR DIARY
or
INTELLIGENCE SUMMARY
(Erase heading not required.)

Instructions regarding War Diaries and Intelligence Summaries are contained in F. S. Regs., Part II. and the Staff Manual respectively. Title Pages will be prepared in manuscript.

Place	Date	Hour	Summary of Events and Information	Remarks and references to Appendices
L'HEURE.	16th	—	1 Sgt. 1 Cpl. S.S. 1 Br. 2 Drs to Hosp. 7 L.D. 1 Mule to M.V.S. 1 R. Dr to I.M.	
	17th	—	7. L.D to M.V.S. rec'd from Base.	
	18	—	4 Brs 1 Dr to Hospital	
	19		1 Br. 1 S.S. to Hospital.	
	21		4 Drs to Hospital. 1 Sr admitted. 1 Sr evacuated	
	22		3 Drs Discharged. 1 Sr admitted. 4 Drs Discharged	
	25th		Captain Hemsworth 1st Reserve Regt Can? joined. 4 Hosp.	
	26		1.Br. 1. S.S. discharged from Hospital. 1 Sgt. 1 Hosp. 2 Gunners ev'acd to Hosp.	
	28		Horses. 20 L.D from Base 1 Cpl to Hospital 2 Drs discharged from Hosp.	
	29th		Administrative. Notification of move rec'd from 1.R.1. R.D from Base	
	31st		Hospital. 2 Drs admitted. 2 L.B. 3 miles to M.V.S.	
			1 Br.	

F.E. Johnston Lt Colonel R.F.A.
O.C. 18. D.A.C.

WAR DIARY or INTELLIGENCE SUMMARY

Army Form C. 2118

18 D. Amm. Col — Vol 17

Place	Date	Hour	Summary of Events and Information	Remarks and references to Appendices
L'HEURE	1.1.17	—	Horses 1 L.D. to M.V.S. 1 Mule to M.V.S. 1 Sergt. to Hospital. 1 Sergt. evacuated.	
GUSCHART	2.1.17	—	Hospital. 1 S.S. admitted. DAC left L'HEURE for forward area.	
	3rd	—	Hospital. 1 Driver admitted. 1 Bdr evacuated. Horses 1 R. 1 L.D. to M.V.S.	
MEZORELLES	3rd	—	Hospital. 1 Bdr. 1 Bdr admitted and evacuated.	
MARIEUX	4th	—	Arrived about 4 pm.	
SENLIS	5th	—	Column arrived 12 Noon. (V.S. C.4.b.) Sheet 57 D.)	
"	6th	—	Officer ½ Lt R.D. Taylor on T.M. Course. One L.D. left at HEIRMONT	
"	7th	—	Hospital. 1 Driver to Hospital. 1 Discharged.	
"	8th	—	Hospital 1 Cpl. 1 Bdr. 1 Bdr. 1 Driver 1 Bdr discharged.	
"	9th	—	1 Corpl. 1 Bdr. 1 S.S. evacuated. Horses 1 L.D. discharged 1. L.D & M.V.S. 1 L.D died.	
"	10th	—	Hospital. 1 Fitter Cpl. 1 S.S. 1 Sadlr. 1 a/Bdr admitted. 1 a/Bdr 1 Sadlr evacuated.	
"	11th	—	2 Drivers discharged.	
"	12th	—	1 Bdr 3 Drivers admitted to Hospital.	
"	13th	—	1 BQMS. 1 a/Bdr 1. Bdr admitted to Hospital. Dr BENGE No 4 Sec: died suddenly	
"	14th	—	1 Bdr & 2 Drs discharged	
"	15th	—	1 L.D. Horse to M.V.S. 2/Lt. H. BARTLETT. 2/Lt Scott joined from Base Depot	
"	16th	—	Officers. 2/Lt C.H. LIDSTONE. 2/Lt H. BARTLETT. 2/Lt Scott reported to proceed to 50th Bn	
"	17th	—	1 Cpl. 1 Bdr 6 Drs admitted to Hospital.	
"	19th	—	2 mules shot. Asst. Vet Officer. 1 Driver admitted.	
"	20th	—	Horses 1 L.D. to M.V.S. 1 Driver admitted.	
"	21st	—	1 Bdr and 3 Drs admitted to Hospital.	
"	22nd	—	2. L.D to M.V.S.	
"	23rd	—	1 Bdr discharged from Hospital.	

WAR DIARY or INTELLIGENCE SUMMARY

Army Form C. 2118

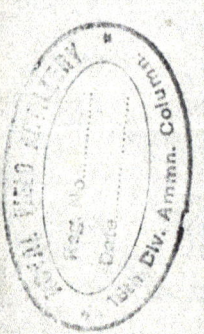

Place	Date	Hour	Summary of Events and Information	Remarks and references to Appendices
New SENLIS	Jan 1917 24th	—	1 Dr admitted. 2 Drs evacuated. Horse C.L.S. admitted. 2 Dr evacuated thro' C.C.S.	
"	25th	—	18. D.A.C. Ammn Col. re-organised to 2 Sections & 73. Echelon. No 3 Section becoming 3rd Army F.A. B.A.C. (Army Troops) 84 Bde, becomes Army F.A. Bde.	
"	26th	—	Horses I.R. 31 Mules from Remount Depot. 2 Drivers to Hospital.	
"	27th	—	1 Anmn discharged.	
"	28th	—	2 Drivers admitted. 1 Br. & Dr. discharged. 2 Dr. evacuated.	
"	29th	—	1 Br. 1 Dr. admitted. 1 Dr. discharged.	
"	30th	—	Hospital 1 Br. evacuated. 1 Dr. discharged. 1 Mule also 1 anK. Vet Officer. 2/Lieut H. Scott to 83rd Bde.	
"	31st	—	Nil.	

J.E. Johnston.
Lieut Colonel R.F.A.
O.C. 18. D.A.C.
31-1-17.

Vol 18

18th D.A.C

Army Form C. 2118

B 284

WAR DIARY
or
INTELLIGENCE SUMMARY
(Erase heading not required.)

Place	Date	Hour	Summary of Events and Information	Remarks and references to Appendices
SENLIS	1st Feb 1917	—	Hospital. 1 Bomb. & 4 Drs admitted.	
	2nd	—	Hospital. 1 Corpl. 1 B.S.M. 1 Sgt. & 2 Drs admitted.	
	3rd	—	Hospital. 1 Dr. admitted.	
	4th	—	Hospital. 1 Dr admitted	
	5th	—	Hospital. 1 Cpl S.S. admitted	
	6th	—	Hospital. 2 Drs evacuated. Horses. One mule to M.V.S.	
	7th	—	" 1 Dr discharged.	
	8th	—	" 1 Dr discharged. 1 Dr admitted. 1 L.D. Horse	
			to M.V.S. Lieut Moss. & 2 Lieut Bartlett to 5th T.M. Course	
			Officers — Three L.D. and 1 mule to M.V.S.	
	9th	—	Hospital. 2 Drivers admitted.	
	10th	—	Hospital. 1 Driver admitted. 1 L.D. to M.V.S.	
	11th	—	Hospital. 1 Saddler admitted. Arrivals. Lt Macrae 1/1st Argyle &	
	12th	—	Hospital. 1 Dr discharged. 2/Lt Stirling admitted.	
	13th	—	" " "	
	14th	—	" 2 Drivers discharged. 1 Dr discharged.	
	15th	—	" 1 Dr. 1 Br. admitted. 1 Dr. to M.V.S. Chaplain Captain Parkinson	
			Horses 15 L.D. 1 M.D. & M.V.S. Chaplain Captain Parkinson joined. Also Captain Thompson 2nd Dragoon Guards.	

1875 Wt. W 593/826 1,000,000 4/15 J.B.C. & A. A.D.S.S./Forms/C. 2118.

Army Form C. 2118

WAR DIARY
or
INTELLIGENCE SUMMARY
(Erase heading not required.)

Instructions regarding War Diaries and Intelligence Summaries are contained in F.S. Regs., Part II. and the Staff Manual respectively. Title Pages will be prepared in manuscript.

Place	Date	Hour	Summary of Events and Information	Remarks and references to Appendices
SENLIS	16	—	Hospital. 2 Brs discharged.	
	17	—	1 Br discharged; 1 S.S. Cpl discharged, 1 Br admitted	
			2/Lt H Bartlett admitted. Hosp. 2 Brs admitted.	
	19	—	Officers joined. Lt W R Carnakan; 2Lt T H Holyoak; 2Lt A E Vantini; Capt W B Daniell.	
	20	—	Hospital. 1 Br 1 Br admitted. 1 Br 1 Br discharged.	
	22		Horses 2 Mules. 2 L.D.H. to M.V.S. 1 L.D.H. sh.P. 4 L.D.H. to M.V.S.	
	23		1 Cpl. 30 Gnrs. 50 Brs to Bac from Base.	
	25		Hosp. 6 Brs admitted and 1 S Smith	
	26		Horses 1 L.D.H. sh.P. 2Lt Vantini to 5th Army Trench School	
	27		Gunners 10 Drivers 6. to 82nd Bde.	
	-"		Gunners 17. -"- 35 to 84 -"-	
	28		Recd instructions to prepare to move to W.6. a sheet 57P	

J Johnston
Lt Colonel R.F.A.
O.C. 18 DAC

Vol 19

War Diary
for
March 1917.

18th Divisional Ammunition
Column.

To,
Officer i/c ~~Corps~~
R.A. & R.A. Records
Headquarters
18th Div Arty

Herewith War Diary for
April 1917 for this Unit.

6/5/17.   [signature] Lieut Col R.A.
              Commanding 18th DAC

Vol 20

War Diary
of
April 1917

18th D.A.C.

Army Form C. 2118

WAR DIARY
or
INTELLIGENCE SUMMARY
(Erase heading not required.)

Instructions regarding War Diaries and Intelligence Summaries are contained in F.S. Regs., Part II. and the Staff Manual respectively. Title Pages will be prepared in manuscript.

Place	Date	Hour	Summary of Events and Information	Remarks and references to Appendices
Authuille	April 1st	—	Horses. Column moved from Senlis to AUTHUILLE.	
	2nd	—	Horses. 13 L.D. and 14 mules to M.V.S.	
	3rd	—	Officers. Captain Jennings & Hunter, attached to 16 D.A.C.	
	4th	—	Hospital. 1 S.S. to Hospital evacuated. 1 Driver to Hospital.	
	5th	—	Horses. 1 L.D. killed by hostile shell fire	
	6th	—	Hospital. 1 Dr. 2 Drivers discharged hospital. 1 R.D. home destroyed.	
	7th	—	Hospital. 2. Dr. admitted.	
	8th	—	Hospital. 2 Drs. discharged.	
	9th	—	Officer. Lt. McCombie posted to X. Trench Mortar Bn.	
	10th	—	Lt. Ricard from 84 B.A.C. joined. Received 79 L.D. and 5 R. from Remount Dept.	
	11th	—	Horses. 1 L.D. destroyed. 1 L.D. posted to 16 D.A.C.	
	12th	—	Officer. Lt Flynn, Griffith, and Love from T.M. Course.	
	13th	—	Lt. Vanter returned from M.V.S.	
	14th	—	Horses - mules - 1 L.S.m	
	15th	—	One L.D. destroyed. 1 mule to M.V.S.	
	16th	—	Horses. 3. L.D. and 2 mules to M.V.S.	
	17th	—	Officer - Lieut A.H. Hobson arrived. No 2 Sec moved to Boom RAVINE	
	18th	—	Horses 5 L.D. from 30th M.V.S. one Dr to Base released from Munitions	
	19th	—	Horses 16. L.D. to M.V.S. Lt Fell, Lt Harvey, Lt Dixon arrived from Base.	
	20th	—	Officers - Lt Cattling. Lt Harvey. 9 Gunners from Base. 61 Gunners, 2 Cpls. 25 Drs 26 Drs to S3 Bde. 2 Sgts. 2 Cpls. 25 Drs 26 Drs to 82 Bde. Lt Harvey to V.15. TMBy	
			3 Sgt. 2 Cpls. 57 Drivers, 61 Gunners from Base. 9 Gunners to V.15. TMBy	
			1 Sgt. 18 Grs. 10 Drs. to 82nd Bde. 2 Sgts. 2 Cpls. 25 Drs. 26 Drs to 83 B4. 1 Driver to Transportation Dept. Boulogne.	

Army Form C. 2118

WAR DIARY
or
INTELLIGENCE SUMMARY

(Erase heading not required.)

Place	Date	Hour	Summary of Events and Information	Remarks and references to Appendices
Authuille	22nd	-	Hospital. 2 Drivers admitted. Horses 2. L.D. & M.V.S.	
	24th	-	Horses 1 L.D. & M.V.S.	
	25th	-	Horses 1 L.D destroyed. 1 L.D. 1 M. & M.V.S.	
RUBEMPRE	26	-	Moves. Authuille to Rubempre. arrived 1pm	
BEAUVAL	27	-	" Column arrived at Beauval. 8pm.	
BEAUVOIR	28	-	" Arrived at 2.30pm.	
RIVIERE	"	-		
AUBROMETZ	29th	-	moves arrived about 3pm. No 2 Sec to MOUCHEL	
BERGUEN BUSE	30th	-	" Column arrived about 2pm. part of column at MAISNIL LES TENEUR.	
FONTES	31st	-	Column moved to FONTES. arrived 2pm. Column rec'd	
	-	-	1 Corps. 1 Bt. 5 Fn. 2. S.S. from Base. Column rec'd orders to move to HAZEBROUCK	

J C Johnston
Lt Colonel RFA
O.C. 18. D.A.C.

Place	Date	Hour	Summary of Events and Information	Remarks and references to Appendices
Hazebrouck	1st	3 pm	Column arrived at Hazebrouck	
			1 Cpl, 1 Sddr, 5 gnrs arrived from Base	
			1 mule destroyed	
	2nd		Horses 1 L.D to M.V.S, 1 L.D destroyed	
			Horses 1 L.D and one mule destroyed	
			3 Drivers admitted to Hospital	
	3rd		9 Gnrs arrived from Base, 7 for the T.M.B's	
	6th		" " " "	
			1 Cpl posted to 82nd Bde and 1 for the Transportation Depot Rouen	
	7th		Horses 2 L.D destroyed 2 V.O.	
			1 Cpl 3 Gnrs 7 Drs posted to 87th Bde	
			2 Sgts 16 Gnrs 1 D.S and Dr to 85th Bde	
			1 Dr admitted to Hospital	
	9th		Horses 1 R. and 1 L.D. 2 mules to M.V.S.	
			100 remounts arrived from Remount Depot Calais	
			Officer Lt. A. Burt to Conflans (under transfer of remounts)	

WAR DIARY
or
INTELLIGENCE SUMMARY

(Erase heading not required.)

Army Form C. 2118

Place	Date	Hour	Summary of Events and Information	Remarks and references to Appendices
Hazebrouck	April 9th		Officers 2nd Lt R.G. Hilton assumed duties of adjutant from this date	
	10th		O.R. discharged from hospital	
			Horses 1 L.D. died and 1 L.D. destroyed by V.O.	
	12th		1 pte admitted to hospital	
			1 O.R. from B one	
	14th		2 O.Rs admitted to hospital	
			Horses 3 L.D. and 4 mules to M.V.S.	
	15th		Officers 2nd Lt Bracken to D.A.C. from B2/P.C.C.	
			2nd Lt Dixon to B/82nd	
			2nd Lt Calthrop to C/82 Bde	
			2nd Lt Margate to [?]	
			2nd Lt Bourke to D.A.C. from 83rd Bde	
			Horses 19 L.D. transferred to B/82	
			8 L.D. and 4 mules to C/82	
			5 mules to D/82	
			3 L.D. to A/83	
			11 mules to B/83	
			3 L.D. to C/83	

Army Form C. 2118

WAR DIARY or INTELLIGENCE SUMMARY

(Erase heading not required.)

Instructions regarding War Diaries and Intelligence Summaries are contained in F.S. Regs., Part II. and the Staff Manual respectively. Title Pages will be prepared in manuscript.

Place	Date	Hour	Summary of Events and Information	Remarks and references to Appendices
Hazebrouck	April 15th		B/82 sent 6 mules to DAC	
			C/82 " 4 mules to DAC	
	17		1 cqpl and 1 Bdr posted to 83rd MB etc	
			1 SS admitted to Hospital	
	18		1 fr 1 Dr admitted to Hospital	
			Horses 3 LD to MVS	
	19		1 Sgt to Hospital	
			Horses 1 LD to MVS	
			1 cqpl arrived from Base	
	20		2 Drs admitted Hospital venereal	
	21		2 Drs to Hospital	
			Horses 1 LD. 5 MVS	
	22		1 fr to Hospital	
			Horses 1 LD to MVS	
			mule orders received	

Army Form C. 2118

WAR DIARY
or
INTELLIGENCE SUMMARY
(Erase heading not required.)

Instructions regarding War Diaries and Intelligence Summaries are contained in F. S. Regs., Part II. and the Staff Manual respectively. Title Pages will be prepared in manuscript.

Place	Date	Hour	Summary of Events and Information	Remarks and references to Appendices
Attigny	June 24		1 Dr returned from Hospital to Unit of "A" E.J., L.M. for ord D.A.C. arrived at "A" Echelon O'Hanghan unfilled men	
	25		"B" " L'éclule 2 Drs and 1 for remounts each Horses 4 L.R. arrived from Remount Depot	
	26		3 Serjts 34 pts 17 Drs arrived from Base Orders to move received 14.0 to M.V.S. 14.0 detained J.V.O. Column moved to "A" Echelon Romainville "B" "	
	27		1 Capt 1 B.S. 4 Drs arrived from Base Column moved to Burguemere "B" "	Hout rinse
	28		1 S.S. returned from Hospital Column arrived to "A" "Echelon to Rubrenville "B" " G Ethel Women	

Army Form C. 2118

WAR DIARY
or
INTELLIGENCE SUMMARY

(Erase heading not required.)

Instructions regarding War Diaries and Intelligence Summaries are contained in F. S. Regs., Part II. and the Staff Manual respectively. Title Pages will be prepared in manuscript.

Place	Date	Hour	Summary of Events and Information	Remarks and references to Appendices
	April 29th		2 Ors to Hospital + unwounded. Horses 2 L D to mVS Column moved to Wailly Horses 3 L D to M.V.S. 2 mules died	
	30th		Column moved to Bavincourt O.mp formed & filled Capt Webster i/c	

J. Johnston
Lieut Colonel, R.E.A.
Comdg 18th D.A. Column

1875 Wt. W593/826 1,000,000 4/15 J.B.C. & A. A.D.S.S./Forms/C. 2118.

War Diary
for
MAY. 1917.
18th D.A.C.

Army Form C. 2118

Instructions regarding War Diaries and Intelligence Summaries are contained in F.S. Regs., Part II. and the Staff Manual respectively. Title Pages will be prepared in manuscript.

WAR DIARY
or
INTELLIGENCE SUMMARY
(Erase heading not required.)

Place	Date	Hour	Summary of Events and Information	Remarks and references to Appendices
BOISLEUX ST. MARC.	1.5.17. 2nd.	—	Capt. W.S. Webster R.F.A. placed in charge of 18th A.R.P. 1 Dr. admitted to hospital.	
	3rd		Artillery Operation Order received and amendments thereto. Large amount of ammunition delivered by Sections in conjunction with above operation order.	
	4th		4 Drivers admitted Hospital. 4 L.D. Horses to M.V.S. 20 Gunners and 22 Drivers from Base Depot. Standard of training of Drivers not good.	
	5th.		Weather during past week hot and fine.	
	7th		One a/Bdr. to Hospital.	
	9th		One L.D. Horse to M.V.S. One Sergt. posted 83rd Bde.	
	10th		1 Driver admitted Hospital.	
	11th		3 L.D. horses to M.V.S.	
	12th		Lieut. T. Genney rejoined from Hospital.	
	14th.		Sections delivered large amounts of ammunition to guns and carried out many R.E. fatigues (material for position vii Corps G.C.R. 810/1 re partial demobilisation of Divisional Artilleries in case of emergency received. Not thought likely to affect this particular Division. 1 Driver discharged from Hospital.	
	15th		18th D.A.C. and Wagon Lines moved to new area. Increased facilities for grazing horses	
BOIRY ST MARTIN	15th		One Driver discharged from horses. One L.D. to M.V.S.	
	16th		Following postings made to Brigades. 82nd. 9 Grs. 12 Drs.	
	18th		To 83rd. 1 Gr. and 5 Drs. Weather continues fine and warm.	
	19th		1 Dr. admitted to hospital and evacuated. Divisional Artillery Horse Rest Camp formed. Capt. E. Bryce Wilson (5th Lancers) Capt. Daniell R.F.A. and Lt. Mac.Nee attached there for duty. Collection and delivery of Tents etc. carried out by this Unit.	

Army Form C. 2118

WAR DIARY
or
INTELLIGENCE SUMMARY
(Erase heading not required.)

Instructions regarding War Diaries and Intelligence Summaries are contained in F.S. Regs., Part II. and the Staff Manual respectively. Title Pages will be prepared in manuscript.

Place	Date	Hour	Summary of Events and Information	Remarks and references to Appendices
BOIRY ST MARTIN	19th		Operation order No 123/A received.	
	20th		2/Lieut. P. Glynn and Lieut. T. Geaney attached A/82nd Bde.	
	21st		5 Sergts. 1 Cpl. and 1 Bdr. from Base.	
	25th		1 Dr. to Hospital. 4 L.D.Horses to M.V.S. R.A. No.J.S. 1/132 received re Brigades withdrawing to Rest Camp for short periods.	
	26th		2/Lieut. H. Bartlett rejoined from Hospital. 2/Lieut. P.J. Shelley attached to C/83rd Brigade. 18th Div. Art Operation Order No 124 received.	
	28th		1 Dr. admitted to Hospital. 1 L.D. to Mobile Vet. Section. Weather continues Hot and fine. 3 L.D.Horses to M.V.S. 1 L.D. Horse destroyed. Up to present date the animals of the unit appear to have benefited greatly from the grazing. Much attention has been given to the overhaul of vehicles, painting them etc. which was greatly needed owing to the amount of fatigues carried out.	
	29th		2 L.D. Horses to M.V.S.	
	30th		18th R.A. No I.S. 1/133 (Defence Scheme) received	
			Generally. During the past month the health of the Column has been particularly good. Admissions to Hospital have been few, and the number reporting sick daily has greatly decreased. Petty crime in the Unit has decreased to minimum. Spray baths have been erected and run by the Unit for the whole of the Divisional Artillery.	

J.C. Johnston
Lieut. Colonel RFA

Vol 22

18th D.A.C.

June 1917

WAR DIARY
or
INTELLIGENCE SUMMARY
(Erase heading not required.)

Army Form C. 2118

Place	Date	Hour	Summary of Events and Information	Remarks and references to Appendices
Bony St Martin	1/6/17	—	On L D to M.V.S	
"	2/6/17	—	1 D² discharged to hospital	
		—	1 pm. ported to B 2nd D.L	
		—	1 L D to M.V.S.	
"	3/6/17	—	2 L D to M.V.S one 11th ported to 23rd F.A. B⁴y	
"	5/6/17	—	D² to Hospital one discharged	
	6/6/17	—	one D² to Camps C pm 7 D² arrived from Base	
		—	5 Surps 4 Camps 6 pm 7 D² arrived from Base	
		—	1 pm ported from hospital F/A 13¹ Div	
	7/6/17	—	2" M A.E. Prichafs and 1" M A.C. Sparks ported from Base	
	8/6/17	—	1 D² to Hospital 4 pm from 82nd D² ported to M.S.	
		"	1" M. I.J Shew — 1" M. E. Mayer — 2" M. J.R. Pyne & 2" M. R.J. Shaw	
	9/6/17	—	passed from Base J Lt. S Doherty invalided to England sick	

WAR DIARY
or
INTELLIGENCE SUMMARY

Army Form C. 2118

Place	Date	Hour	Summary of Events and Information	Remarks and references to Appendices
Army S.C. Mauritius	9/6/17	—	1 L.D. to M.V.S.	
"	10/6/17	—	2nd Lt Duhigg and 2nd Lt Page attached to 87 2 B.G. on B.G. and 9 Syces to 87 and B.G. 2 pers to 83rd Hy on L.D. to M.V.S.	
"	11/6/17	—	1 Syce to hospital	
	12/6/17	—	1 Syce to 56 A.S.P. and 1 Syce N/18 T.m. 5 L.D. to M.V.S.	
	13/6/17		one D.R. to hospital Capt Newell to England sick 8 Syces and O.R. return from Pool	
	14/6/17	—	1 L.D. to M.V.S.	
	15/6/17	—	1 Capt to Hospital	
	17/6/17		1 Officer discharged from hospital	
	18/6/17		3 Syces to 87 2nd B.G. and 4 pers 10th to 83rd Hy	

Army Form C. 2118

WAR DIARY
or
INTELLIGENCE SUMMARY
(Erase heading not required.)

Instructions regarding War Diaries and Intelligence Summaries are contained in F. S. Regs., Part II. and the Staff Manual respectively. Title Pages will be prepared in manuscript.

Place	Date	Hour	Summary of Events and Information	Remarks and references to Appendices
Bray St Martin	20/6/17	—	1 L.D. to match Vet Sect	
"	22/6/17		3 L.D to M.V.S.	
	23/6/17		75 OR and 16 ft horses from Base	
	26/6/17		2 to H L Normandy to hospital and 1 OR from A/280	
	27/6/17		and OR to hospital	
	28/6/17		2 L D to M.V.S.	
	29/6/17		1 OR to hospital	
	30/6/17		1 OR to Hospital	

During this month the horses of 1 & 2 N.C. benefited greatly from good grazing in the neighbourhood

R. J. Melling
Capt & V
for O.C. 13th D.A.C.

Officer i/c RA & RFA Records H45

Headquarters
18th Divl Artillery

Herewith War Diary for July 1917.

R. G. Hilton Capt RFA for
Lieut Col RFA
Commdg 18th D.A.C.

WAR DIARY or INTELLIGENCE SUMMARY

Army Form C. 2118.

18 D Am Col
Vol 23

Place	Date	Hour	Summary of Events and Information	Remarks and references to Appendices
Berg St Martin	3/7/17	3	Orders to move received	
		4	Column moved to Ackemuth. Left 9.30 am	
		5	Very wet morning, arrived about 3 pm	
		6	Column moved to Fauchin via St Pol and remained there one day	
		7	March continued to Nidely and Niderville left about 6 am	
		8	Column marched to In Cansiene & Beveghem between St Milaine and Hayternck	
		9	Marched to Staple area of Hayternck. 27 W.S Rotherham joined from A/18 NHA (drawn here opened to commissions in the field promotal duties)	
		10	Left start 4 am & marched to Each area Hazefra in Esther huts, Enemy army out	

WAR DIARY
or
INTELLIGENCE SUMMARY

Army Form C. 2118.

Place	Date	Hour	Summary of Events and Information	Remarks and references to Appendices
Funka	1/7/17		Column marched to new lines between Dickebusch and Ouderdom. H 26 A and C.	
H 26 a & c 12	12		Commenced to dig in down to the four foot.	
	13		Further casualties shelling. 1 gr wounded return detained. Further casualties during shown by gun. Further says that shelled Jan. 7 H E shells. 2 O.D killed. 1 wounded 6 horses killed.	
	14		Again heavy casualties during time by gun. 2 officers wounded 3 men killed 6 wounded. 19 animals killed and 11 wounded & missing. Column at this period was rolled upon to deliver very large amount of amm which it eventually carried out in spite of the fact that very many R.E wagon trying was also done nightly. R.E material etc to the gun position to the advanced posts. Draft from the 11 and 4 D.D	

A6943 Wt. W14422/M1160 339,000 12/16 D.D.&L. Forms/C/2118/4.

WAR DIARY
or
INTELLIGENCE SUMMARY.

Army Form C. 2118.

Place	Date	Hour	Summary of Events and Information	Remarks and references to Appendices
H 26 a	14/7/17		a/B a Anjou, 2 Lieut Munn and Capt Beith with an attached VIII Division moved for guard duty when return time to 17th Army.	
			Much confused shuffling	
	15		Again say lines visit column up steam	
	16		2 Hornburk, 2 Lt Thompson & Lt Parry arrived from Base	
			Forge around O6 taken up to from 8 forge and 2 PD posted to 82 two B Cy 5 fd and 8 PD 23rd B Cy	
	19		Instructions arrived re starting horseshoe	
	21st		From Base 1 Sergt 1 Shr Army Amount G.H.Q.R delivered at first 42 LD and 10 mules attached from B Cy and 25 LD, 82 B Cy and 24 LD to B3rd B Cy	
	22nd		2 Lt Ferra to first reinforcement from Signals School	

WAR DIARY
or
INTELLIGENCE SUMMARY
(Erase heading not required.)

Army Form C. 2118

Place	Date	Hour	Summary of Events and Information	Remarks and references to Appendices
#26a	22/7/17		Successfully delivered ammunition 15 A.A to which haled to the dumps in Zillebeke church which was to the 8.3" 6" 1" 15 & 2" D.a. 4 pm	
			D.A.C. huns shelled with 5.9 about 3 pm Holy 6 huns " " " 6 pm North was early got off the limber	
	23		Column moved to H 32 c 5.5 near the wood 1 St Anterlinck 1 D" wounded man wounded while delivery ammn.	
	24		6 ammns killed & wounded. Female and empty Pack Sub were Attmer by the D.A.C. It mules were left of the female & S.A.A Sent 60 pack mules of the Supply Pack Sent forward with 64 pack mules of ammns from the Butts	

Army Form. C. 2118

WAR DIARY
or
INTELLIGENCE SUMMARY
(Erase heading not required.)

Place	Date	Hour	Summary of Events and Information	Remarks and references to Appendices
A32 c	25/7/17		Enemy trenches again shelled during 2 P.D. killed 8 wounded & missing. Large amount of ammunition was detonated 2 R.C. army wounded 2 men wounded 21 horses killed & wounded obtaining ammn	
	26		2 M Sharp started 82 "B" Co " " Lothian " A/83 2 " Brighton " A/82	
	27		Bombs were dropped on Camp killing 2 men wounded 3 and killed 21 animals and wounded 13 6 horses wounded & missing while detaining ammn From 15 mm 1 bugl. 15 /em 28 PD	

Army Form. C. 2118

WAR DIARY
or
INTELLIGENCE SUMMARY
(Erase heading not required.)

Instructions regarding War Diaries and Intelligence Summaries are contained in F. S. Regs., Part II. and the Staff Manual respectively. Title Pages will be prepared in manuscript.

Place	Date	Hour	Summary of Events and Information	Remarks and references to Appendices
H 32 c	28/7/17		Posted to 82nd R.F.A 39 [?] and 38 [?] to 83rd R.F.A	
	29/7/17		Heavy quantities of ammn delivered to guns. From Rose 16 fm 8.0 f. 7 Howitzer journal from Rose	
	31st		A R.P. moved to forward area at N. Notan [?] from the Base. During this month the D.A.C has been either engaged in collecting delivering a very large amount of ammunition to the firing positions under very heavy exceptional circumstances. This amounts to 18 waggon trips in a handy shelled & gassed area has thrown a great strain on the personnel of the D.A.C attended with many casualties.	

Signed
Lieut. Colonel, R.F.A
Comdg 18th Div. Amm. Column.

WAR DIARY
or
INTELLIGENCE SUMMARY

18th A.C.

Army Form C. 2118.

Place	Date	Hour	Summary of Events and Information	Remarks and references to Appendices
# 32 C N of Mishah	1/8/17		7th A.A.C. arrived in this Camp until the 30th of this month when orders were received to move to Jerusalem No 1 canal. to which place on O.A.C. watched the same day. During the whole period previous to this move my Band with us down to all Sorts in delivering exam and of the area have never seen been either empty from perchance. No 2 Sect received most men Kabyia delivering R.E. material to Tumsah area.	
	3/8/17		The following officers joined from this Base: 2/Lt T want, 2/Lt Stewart and S with	

WAR DIARY
or
INTELLIGENCE SUMMARY.

Army Form C. 2118.

Place	Date	Hour	Summary of Events and Information	Remarks and references to Appendices
H.Q. 2	3/8/17		2nd Lt A. Wickson & 2nd Lt H. Parker joined Battalion	
	15/8/17		2nd Lt Jenny, 2nd Lt Baker & 2nd Lt Dowell, 2nd Lt Raley, 2nd Lt Walsh, 2nd Lt Jn Wilson, 2nd Lt Waddle, 2nd Lt J. Bullard.	
	21/8/17		2nd Lt H Hall, 2nd Lt H.S. Tanner & 2nd Lt W Winder, 2nd Lt S D Cooper & 2nd Lt J Bostock.	
	26/8/17		2nd Lt Hutchinson and 2nd H Berry posted to O.T.C. from 8 3rd Bn. The following 2 O.R's joining from Base	
	1/9/17		1 O.R. 3 Sep, 8 O.R.	
	9/8/17		15 September 4 5 July 18 O.R.	

WAR DIARY
or
INTELLIGENCE SUMMARY

Army Form C. 2118.

Place	Date	Hour	Summary of Events and Information	Remarks and references to Appendices
H32c	10/8/17	4 OR		
		5- Shrapnel		
	13/2/17	1 Sgt 15 ORs		Killed & fell from 2.5
		1 Capt, 1 R & C 41 ORs		Wounded 3 3
	13 "	1 Sergt		To M.V.S. 4 8
	19 "			Received from Base 7 & 5
	28 "	To Infantry ORs		were posted to B Coy
	8/8/17	To B Coy 15 dt	from B Coy
		4 dt	9 OR	17
		To B & N dt		
	4/8/17	28 "	1 Sgt 2 Coys & 15 ORs 15/8 25	This 42/19
	8/8/17	18 " 20 OR		
	8/8/17	Lt. E.R. Smith wounded whilst taking up S.A.A to infantry		
	4/8/17	Capt W. Webster posted to O/3 B		

Army Form C. 2118.

WAR DIARY
or
INTELLIGENCE SUMMARY.
(Erase heading not required.)

Instructions regarding War Diaries and Intelligence Summaries are contained in F. S. Regs., Part II. and the Staff Manual respectively. Title pages will be prepared in manuscript.

Place	Date	Hour	Summary of Events and Information	Remarks and references to Appendices
#52			The following officers were posted to 75 dn:	
			2 Lt D Powell to B 2" 75 dn	
			2 Lt " Wistar " " "	
			2 Lt H.W.Brown " " "	
			2 Lt J M Watson " " "	
	24/8/17		2 Lt J G Skinner " " "	
			2 Lt A R Payne " " "	
			2 Lt J Gunn " " "	
			2 Lt A Bartlett " " "	
			2 Lt A S Sharp " " "	
	27/8/17		2 Lt H J Hobson to B 3 "" 75 dn	
			2 Lt M S Mulhollam " " "	
			2 Lt W J Bolan " " "	
			2 Lt R R F... " " "	

R.J. Mullin Capt
Comdg 1st Div Ammn Column R.F.A.
for

WAR DIARY
or
INTELLIGENCE SUMMARY.

(Erase heading not required.)

18th D.A.C.

Army Form C. 2118.

/R 25

Place	Date	Hour	Summary of Events and Information	Remarks and references to Appendices
OUDEZEELE	1-9-17		Column was at rest in this area. Following officers joined unit from Base Depôt, 7½ o'clock. 2/Lt R.S. Ellis, 2/Lt W.McIntosh, and 2/Lt H.I. Moore.	
"	2-9-17		8 Sergeants from IInd Corps joined for posting to Brigades of 18 Div R.A. 2 L.D. animals evacuated to M.V.S. 140 destroyed.	
"	3-9-17		2/Lt W.B. Stirling rejoined unit from CORDOVA DUMP. Lt R.B. Munn joined from II Corps. Following postings and attachments:— To 54th Brigade 4 Sergeants, 2 Shoeing Smiths, 5 Gunners, 8 Drivers. HQ H. Wilson attached 82nd Brigade. To 83rd Brigade 4 Sergeants, 1 Bombardier, 5 Gunners, 3 Drivers. 2/Lieut Bostock posted to 4" Cavalry Division. During the period 31-9-17 to 4-9-17 an enormous effort was made to overhaul all vehicles, harness etc. and generally clean up after the period in the line (which had been very strenuous).	
"	4-9-17		1 Driver to Hospital sick.	
"	6-9-17		2/Lt J.M. Wilson and 2/Lt W.G.Bannell attached 82nd Brigade.	
"	7-9-17		1 Saddler to Hospital. 1 Driver evacuated through C.C.S.	
"	8-9-17		3 L.D. animals evacuated to M.V.S. 2/Lieut S.B. Cooper attached 83rd Brigade.	

Army Form C. 2118.

WAR DIARY
or
INTELLIGENCE SUMMARY.
(Erase heading not required.)

Instructions regarding War Diaries and Intelligence Summaries are contained in F. S. Regs., Part II. and the Staff Manual respectively. Title pages will be prepared in manuscript.

Place	Date	Hour	Summary of Events and Information	Remarks and references to Appendices
OUDEZEELE	9.9.17		Following re-inforcements received from Base, 7/c Lieutenant 19 Drivers and 1 Farrier	
"			2 Y.S. Horses 14 mules received from Calais	
"			3 L.D. Horses to M.V.S. (sick) 120 Hors(?) to D/153rd Bde	
"	10.9.17		Following officers posted from Base Depot. Lieut J. Bartholomew B.S.R.	
			Henry & Lieut C. Clark	
			2 Drivers 1 Gr. posted from Base. 1 Driver to Hospital sick 1 Farrier discharged	
			11 Drivers 33 Gunners to 82nd Brigade 1 Farrier Sms 29 Gunners and	
			3 Drivers to 83rd Brigade —	
"	11.9.17			
"	12.9.17		1 L.D. to M.V. Section.	
"	13.9.17		2 L.D. to M.V. Section	
"	14.9.17		2 Drivers reported from Hospital	
"	15.9.17		1 Bombardier 1 G. to Hospital	
"	17.9.17		2 Gunners 9 Drivers posted from Base	
"	18.9.17		2 Horses & Mules received from M.V.S.	
"	19.9.17		1 L.D. to M.V.S. 8 Gunners from Base	
			Orders received to evacuate OUDEZEELE AREA and move to SERQUES giving to AREA being required by re-inforcement Units —	

Army Form C. 2118.

WAR DIARY
or
INTELLIGENCE SUMMARY.

(Erase heading not required.)

Instructions regarding War Diaries and Intelligence Summaries are contained in F. S. Regs., Part II. and the Staff Manual respectively. Title pages will be prepared in manuscript.

Place	Date	Hour	Summary of Events and Information	Remarks and references to Appendices
SERQUES.	20-9-17		COLUMN left Dickebusch and arrived SERQUES about 7.30 p.m.	
"	21-9-17		1 Driver to Hospital. 1 Sergeant & Gunner from Base	
"			3 LD Horses received from H.Q. R.G. 10 Divisions	
"	22-9-17		4 Sergeants 8 Corporals 4 Bombardiers received from Base	
"			1 LD Horse destroyed	
"	23-9-17		1 O.R. Hospital. 4 Sergeants 6 Corporals 1 Bombardier 1 Gunner 2 Drivers	
"			to R.F.A. Brigade	
"			Orders received to march into line. Billet first night at	
"			ERINGHEM	
"	24-9-17		Column moved to ERINGHEM. arrived about 3 p.m.	
ERINGHEM	25-9-17		Column left ERINGHEM and marched to PESELHOEK	
PESELHOEK	28-9-17		Orders received to take over camp of H.8. R.A.C. and all S.A.A. Limbered	
			Camps to taken over &500 moved in	
H.Z.A. 6+4 A.28.d.3.6 A.22.a.1.y (Sheet 28 N.W.)	29-9-17		Ammunition supply started. 1 O/R. 1 st Killed, 4 wounded.	
			5. O.R.s wounded	
			Enemy aircraft over camp. Large number of bombs dropped. 2+0 Horses	
			killed 5 wounded.	
			3+0 Horses received from 1st Reginal 64	

Army Form C. 2118.

WAR DIARY
or
INTELLIGENCE SUMMARY.
(Erase heading not required.)

Place	Date	Hour	Summary of Events and Information	Remarks and references to Appendices
Camp near VLAMERTINGHE	30/9/17		2 LD Horses wounded 1 OR to hospital sick **Generally** During the period 1-9-17 to 20-9-17 the 18th D.A.C. was at rest and the time was employed in a general overhaul of vehicles, re & refitting with personnel, and animals. Several sports were arranged mounted gymkhana, and Bde Artillery football tournament. Much benefit was derived from this rest. The Bde. moved back into the line at the latter end of the month. There was a good decrease in the number of sick and hospital cases. On arrival in camp near VLAMERTINGHE the Bde. arcraft have reqd. bombing raids owing to night being fine & moon at full.	

J.C. Johnston
Lieut Colonel R.A.
Comm[ading] 18 Bde Army[?]
Brigade

~~18TH DIVISIONAL ARTILLERY.~~

18TH DIV: AMMN: COLUMN.

WAR DIARY

- FOR -

MONTH OF OCTOBER, 1917.

WAR DIARY or INTELLIGENCE SUMMARY.

Army Form C. 2118.

V 26

Place	Date	Hour	Summary of Events and Information	Remarks and references to Appendices
DAC Wagon Lines near VLAMERTINGHE	1-10-17		Column in position at N.2.a.6.4. (Sheet 28) near VLAMERTINGHE. Lieut. J. Bartholomew posted to 83rd Brigade. One Sergeant posted from Base. 2 L.D. Horses evacuated to M.V.S. 2. O.R. to Hospital.	
	2nd		Enemy aircraft over camps, no casualties. Lieut. W. Winter posted to 83rd Brigade. 3 Sergeants and 3 Corporals to 82nd Brigade. 1 Corporal & Driver posted to 83rd Bde. Enemy aircraft again over camps, number of bombs dropped but no casualties on DAC.	
	3rd		1 O.R. to hospital sick. 2 L.D. Horses to M.V.S.	
	4th		Hostile aircraft again active.	
	5th		1 Driver to hospital.	
	6th		2/Lieut A. S. Robertson posted to DAC (in exchange for W. Winter) from 83rd Brigade. 2/Lieut J. Young posted from Base. 5 L.D. Horses to M.V.S. 2 L.D. Horses killed. 1 wounded.	
	7th		2 O.R. wounded while delivering ammunition to gun positions.	

WAR DIARY or INTELLIGENCE SUMMARY

Army Form C. 2118.

Place	Date	Hour	Summary of Events and Information	Remarks and references to Appendices
D.A.C. WAGON LINES Nr. VLAMERTINGHE.	8/10/17.		2 O.R. to Hospital sick. 1 L.D. Horse to M.V.S. 2 L.D.H. missing. During period 1-8" Oct the following amounts of ammunition were conveyed to gun positions. 10328 - 18pr. 2945. 4·5" how. under very difficult circumstances, as enemy shelled approaches to Battery positions very intensely. "B" Echelon engaged in salving ammunition, guns, vehicles &c.	
	9"		1 L.D. killed.	
	10"		2 O.R. to Hospital. 3 L.D. missing. 4 L.D. wounded.	
	11"		5 L.D. received from Calais. In evening enemy aircraft over camp, bombs were dropped but no casualties.	
			1 O.R. to Hospital sick. 1 Driver from Base. 1 L.D. to M.V.S.	
	12"		18th Divisional Artillery Group Order No. 1 received. 1 R. Horse killed, 2 L.D. wounded on lines by bomb. Enemy aircraft over camp, bombs dropped 2 horses evacuated. 2/Lieut H.P. Donnelly from Base.	
	13"		Following N.C.O.'s & men awarded Military Medal for gallantry and devotion to duty in action. 34191 Dr. J. Gilbert 2658g Farr. Serg. J. Hopper J. 146890 Dr. Williamson R.J. 34398/Saddler Sgt. Trevor D.	

Army Form C. 2118.

WAR DIARY
or
INTELLIGENCE SUMMARY.
(Erase heading not required.)

Instructions regarding War Diaries and Intelligence Summaries are contained in F. S. Regs., Part II. and the Staff Manual respectively. Title pages will be prepared in manuscript.

Place	Date	Hour	Summary of Events and Information	Remarks and references to Appendices
WAGON LINES Nr VLAMERTINGHE	13"		09613 Sergt Wells. F. 38605 Sergt Bagwell G. 1-D died.	
	14"		2/Lieut S.H. Jackson evacuated sick. 3 -1-D to M.V.S. 1 L.D. destroyed.	
	15"		18' Divisional Group order no 4 received 2 t.D wounded. Following amount of ammunition delivered during week 8 - 15"Oct 18 pdr 8190 rds 4x5 3012 rds.	
	16'		1 O.R to Hospital. 10 Gunners posted to T.M's on return from 14 days course at Fifth Army School.	
	17"		2/Lieut A.F. Ellis posted to 8/83. 2/Lt W McIntosh and 2/Lt C Clarke posted to TM's but remaining attached to 18'D.A.C	
	18"		2 O.Rs wounded (1 subsequently died) Following N.C.O's and men awarded Military medal for gallantry and devotion to duty in action 344 Sergt Mules W. 93159 Sergt Mules F.C 42571 D. Foster N. 29953 D. Hancock. F.	

Army Form C. 2118.

WAR DIARY
of
INTELLIGENCE SUMMARY.
(Erase heading not required.)

Place	Date	Hour	Summary of Events and Information	Remarks and references to Appendices
WAGON LINES Mt ILAMERTINGHE. 19"	18"		18" Divisional Artillery Operation order No 4 received	
	20"		3 Drivers received from Base. 18" Div Arty Operation order No 10 received. 2/Lieut WF Smith posted to D/82. 1 O.R. to Hospital.	
	21st		Attached to 18" Div Art Group order 130 received. 2 Sergeants 2 Corporals 2 Bombardiers received from Base. Following ammunition delivered during period 15" - 22nd Oct 18Pr 4045 rds 4x5. 1204 rds.	
	22nd			
	23rd		1 Driver to Hospital. 1 H.D. destroyed. 2 L.D. missing. 1 H.D. drowned.	
	24"		2 Sergts 10 Gunners posted from Base. 2 S.S. 10 Drivers from Base. 1 Serg. 10 Corporals posted to 83rd Brigade. 2 Cpls from 15" Hussars transferred from 11" Hussars transferred to Royal Artillery	
	25"		Rev O.M. Collins to 5"6" B.C.S. Rev D Walker joined.	
	26"		1 Gunner to Hospital wounded. 4 Sergts. H.2. Gunners to Base.	

Army Form C. 2118.

WAR DIARY
or
INTELLIGENCE SUMMARY.
(Erase heading not required.)

Instructions regarding War Diaries and Intelligence Summaries are contained in F. S. Regs., Part II. and the Staff Manual respectively. Title pages will be prepared in manuscript.

Place	Date	Hour	Summary of Events and Information	Remarks and references to Appendices
WAGON LINES NEAR VLAMERTINGHE	28"		1 Gunner to Hospital wounded. 2/Lieut E. Clarke to Hospital wounded	
	29"		1 O.R. discharged from Hospital. 64 Gunner 15 Driver 1 Smith from Base. 9 Gunners 1 Driver (Signaller) from Base. Following amounts of ammunition delivered to Battery previous from 22nd to 29. Oct. 18 pr - 13514 rds. 4"x5" 3105 rds. Capt Randall R.A.M.C. posted to 82nd Brigade.	
	30"		2 Drivers to Hospital sick. 1 R.S. destroyed. 2/Lieut R.W. Forrest from Base. Lt. E.E. Brigman (U.S.M.O.R.C.) joined. Enemy aircraft over during night and camp bombed. Probably one English machine was used (by sound of engine) about 10 planes in all. 4 L.D.M. killed and 3 wounded.	
	31st		Lieut J. Parsons U.S.M.O.R.C. joined. 2/Lieut R.W. Forrest to 73rd Brigade. 4 Sergts. 29 Gunners 5 Drivers to 82nd Brigade. 18 Gunners 11 Drivers to 83rd Brigade.	

WAR DIARY
INTELLIGENCE SUMMARY

Army Form C. 2118.

Place	Date	Hour	Summary of Events and Information	Remarks and references to Appendices
WAGON LINES near VLAMERTINGHE	31st October 1917		**Generally** During the month a great deal of work was done by the unit. Approximately 69,000 rounds of ammunition were delivered to Battery positions during a month. During the first 14 days of the month 3553 rounds of ammunition and 99.91 wagon loads of shell cases were carried from forward areas. The ammunition dump at ZOUAVE VILLA near ST JEAN has been worked by the 18"B.A.C. and large quantities of R.E. material have been collected and distributed by "B" Echelon of the unit. During the latter part of the month a further 1461 rounds of ammunition were carried. 15 Limbered G.S. wagons were detached at the 18th Divisional Bomb Store and S.A.A. & Grenades	

WAR DIARY
or
INTELLIGENCE SUMMARY.
(Erase heading not required.)

Army Form C. 2118.

Place	Date	Hour	Summary of Events and Information	Remarks and references to Appendices
WAGON LINES NEAR YLAMERTINGHE	[?] to 3/2		were detailed to Infantry under the most trying conditions. Casualties have been comparatively light in personnel thanks slightly heavier, owing to a bad roads by Enemy aircraft. Owing to mud and bad roads in forward areas a number of vehicles have had to be abandoned with little hope of them being salved in some cases the mud having practically buried them this combined with intense hostile artillery fire made salving a work of great difficulty. With the assistance of personnel from other details a considerable number of guns were salved and taken to Ordnance Workshops for overhaul. The number of daily sick in on the kind is also on the decrease.	

Army Form C. 2118.

WAR DIARY
or
INTELLIGENCE SUMMARY.
(Erase heading not required.)

Place	Date	Hour	Summary of Events and Information	Remarks and references to Appendices
WAGGON LINES NEAR VLAMERTINGHE	31st		The standard of training of reinforcements received during month is good, and a number have been posted to Brigades of the Divisional Artillery. Taking the month generally the work carried out has been satisfactory.	

J E Johnston
Lieut Col RFA
Commanding 18th Bde Cdn Arty

8/11/17.

WAR DIARY or INTELLIGENCE SUMMARY

Army Form C. 2118.

18th D.A.C.

Vol 27

Place	Date	Hour	Summary of Events and Information	Remarks
H.2.a.6.4. VLAMERTINGHE	1/11/17 to 30/11/17		**OFFICERS**	

The following officers joined on the dates shown against their names:-

2/11/17 2/Lieut H. HUGHES   2/Lt J.M. LIGHT-BODY   2/Lt H.A. CLIST
6/11/17 2/Lieut T. FOSTER   2/Lt H.J. PEACH   2/Lt W. MARLOW   2/Lt A.M. LOWE   2/Lt J.A. BROWN
7/11/17 2/Lieut D. Galbraith   2/Lieut L.B. Smith   2/Lieut G.R. Thompson
9/11/17 2/Lieut J.A. Wright   Capt. J.D. Bathgate   Major Capt. G.A. Prentice   2/Lieut
         C. O'Keefe   2/Lieut 6.S. Downey   2/Lieut T.W.G. Algate   2/Lieut J. Davies
         2/Lieut J.Z.H. Pollen   2/Lieut W.S. Thomas   29/11/17 2/Lieut R.M. Jones 2/Lieut
         6.A. Smith   Capt. B.S. Hogan.   Capt. S.W. Follit (Returned Services)
         Capt. W.B. Savidle.

Following Posting of Officers from DAC were made:
Lieut B.E. Bergmann to 82nd Bde. 1/11/17   2/Lieut Higginbotham 2/Lieut H Hughes
to 83rd Brigade on 2/11/17   Capt C D Rutherford to 82nd Brigade 10/11/17
2/Lieut W.J. Darnell died 2/11/17. 2/Lt J.M. Wilson to 82nd Bde 6/11/17   2/Lieut R J Travers to 83rd
Bde 6/11/17   Capt A.A. Prentice to 82nd Brigade on 11/11/17 2/Lieut F.A.J. Wright to
83rd 11/11/17   2/Lieut W.J. Thomas to 82nd Bde 13-11-17   2/Lieut J. Kennie to 83rd Bde
15/11/17   2/Lieut J.W.G. Algate to 82nd Brigade 12/11/17. 2/Lieut W. Marlow to 82nd Bde
24/11/17.   Following attachments to Brigades were made:-
2/Lieut H.A. Clist to 82nd 3/11/17   2/Lieut J.D. Smith to 83rd 10/11/17   2/Lieut D.
Rutherford to 83rd 16-11-17   2/Lieut N.J. Peach to B/82nd Bde 29/11/17 2/Lieut A.M. Lowe
to 83rd Bde 16/11/17   Capt R.S. Hogan att 82nd Bde 22-11-17.   2/Lieut E.S.
Downey to 82nd Brigade 29-11-17.

Army Form C. 2118.

WAR DIARY
or
INTELLIGENCE SUMMARY.
(Erase heading not required.)

Instructions regarding War Diaries and Intelligence Summaries are contained in F. S. Regs., Part II. and the Staff Manual respectively. Title pages will be prepared in manuscript.

Place	Date	Hour	Summary of Events and Information	Remarks and references to Appendices
M.I.A. G.H. VLAMERTINGHE (SHEET 28.N.W.)	1/11/17		**Hospital** During the month the following were admitted to Hospital:— 2 Shoeing Smiths 1 Bombardier & 2/Boms? 12 Gunners 22 Drivers and were disposed of as follows:— Evacuated to C.C.S. 2 Shoeing Smiths 1 Bom? 2/3/11/17 11 Grs 15 Drivers Returned Unit 1 Gunner 1 Driver 1 Driver Still in hospital.	
			Reinforcements Following reinforcements have been received from Base:— 2/11/17 2 Drivers 20 Drivers. 5/11/17 61 Gunners 6/11/17 62 Gunners 27/11/17 4 Drivers 28/11/17 4 Corporals 3 Fitters Following postings to Brigades made:— 3/11/17 to 82nd Bdespack 6 Drivers to 83rd Brigade. 13 Drivers 7/11/17 4 Stant Brigade 4 Drivers 8/11/17 82nd Bde. 2 Sergts. 3 Corporals 3 Bombrs 80 Gunners 19 Drivers 11/11/17 to 83rd Bde 12 Gunners to 83rd Brigade 20 Gunners 21/11/17 to 82nd Brigade 1 Sergeant 6 Drivers 1 Gunner 24/11/17 to 82nd Brigade 3 Corporals 2 Fitters to 83rd Brigade 4 Corporals 1 Fitter 28/11/17 29 Gunners to J.M. Ballew.	
			Horses Casualties to horses were as follows:— Died. 3 LD. to Mobile Vet. Section. 1 Rider 4 OLD. Killed 4 LD. Escaped 4 LD	

(5050) W. W.22593/M1593. 75 v. 6. 4/17. D.D. & L., Ltd. Forms/C.2118/14.

Army Form C. 2118.

WAR DIARY
or
INTELLIGENCE SUMMARY.
(Erase heading not required.)

Place	Date	Hour	Summary of Events and Information	Remarks and references to Appendices
H.2.a.6.b. VLAMERTINGHE (Sheet 28.N.W.)	1/11/17		Ammunition. Approximately 21,000 rds 18/pr and 4500 rds H×E Ammunition were issued to Battery position during month.	
	30/11/17		Reorganization. On the 21st the Column was reorganised in accordance with "War Establishment No 642. (B.A.C. France) Surplus animals and majority of personnel absorbed into Brigades. Honours & Awards. Lt. B.W. Tubing Awarded Military Cross 5/11/17 for gallantry and devotion to duty in the field Lieut A.R. Turner Awarded Military Cross 15/11/17 for gallantry and devotion to duty in the field –	

F.C. Johnston
Lieut. Colonel. R.F.A.
Comdg 18th Div. Amm. Column

WAR DIARY
or
INTELLIGENCE SUMMARY.
(Erase heading not required.)

Army Form C. 2118.

18 D. Amm. Col. Vol 2 B

Place	Date	Hour	Summary of Events and Information	Remarks and references to Appendices
Vinegon Farm near VLAMERTINGHE.	1st to 15.		**OFFICERS.** The following Officers joined during the month:—	
			Nee. Bnd. — 2/Lt. P. Hamersoli; 2/Lt. W.H. Currie; 2/Lt. W.O. Farmer; 2/Lt. D. Battersbee;	
			" 10th — 2/Lt. F. Gough; 2/Lt. J.I. Dutton;	
	12th		" 22nd. — 2/Lt. L.C. Bottoms	
			" — 2/Lt. H. Wilson.	
			The following officers were attached to Brigades as shewn:—	
			To 82nd. Bde. 2/Lt. F. Gough; J.S. Dutton; R.Q.M. Jones;	
CROMBEKE	13th to 31st.		To 83rd. Bde. 2/Lt. D. Battersbee; W.H. Currie; W.O. Farmer; P. Hamersoli;	
			" 2nd To D.T.M.O. 2/Lt. J. Walker; C.A.H. Smith; E.B. Thompson;	
			Hospital. During the month the following ranks were admitted to Hospital and were disposed of as follows:—	
			1. Sergt. 1. Shr. Smith. 1. Vr. Bnr. 9 Driver 2 Br. to duty;	
			1. Cor. Rec. 9 6 Driver evacuated. 1 Sgt. 16 duty;	
			1. B.S. 15 duty.	
			Reinforcements The following reinforcements were received from Base and	
			26 Grs. 38. Dn. arr. 4-12-17.	
			The following were posted to Brigades.	
			To 82nd/Bde. 2-12-17. 2. Sgs. 2 Sgls. 1 Bnr. 14 Driver	
			To 83rd. Bde. 2-12-17 18. Drivers	

WAR DIARY
or
INTELLIGENCE SUMMARY.
(Erase heading not required.)

Place	Date	Hour	Summary of Events and Information	Remarks and references to Appendices
			Reinforcement contd.	
			To Stud. Bde. 4-12-17. 2/Lt. Gunners.	
			To 83rd Bde 4-12-17. 9 Gunners.	
			From Base 12-12-17. 6. 295.	
			" 13-12-17. 5. Sgts. 53. Gunners.	
			From 83rd Bde & Bac 10-12-17. 20 Drivers 20 Drivers sent to 83rd Bde.	
			" " " " in exchange	
			83rd " " " 15 Drivers 15 Drivers " " 83 "	
			" " " " in exchange	
			To Stud. Bde. 11-12-17. 4. Sgts.	
			To 357. Div. 10-12-17. 6 Drivers	
			To 83rd Bde. 14-12-17. 2. Sgts.	
			" " " 16-12-17. 36 Gunners 9 Drivers	
			" 83rd " 16-12-17. 15 Gunners 6 Drivers	
			" 296 " 28-12-17. 24 Drivers	
			From Base. 24-12-17. 1 Dr. (Posted to 19.R.A.M.D. under age)	
			To Stud. Bde. 24-12-17. 2. Gunners.	
			To 83rd Bde 24-12-17. 1 Sgt. 1. Cpl.	
			From 83rd Bde & Bac 30-12-17. 1 Sgt.	

WAR DIARY
or
INTELLIGENCE SUMMARY.
(Erase heading not required.)

Place	Date	Hour	Summary of Events and Information	Remarks and references to Appendices
			ANIMALS. Casualties to animals during the month were as follows:-	
			To M.V.S. 13 L.D. DESTROYED. 24 L.D. LOST. 1 L.D.	
			AMMUNITION. From Dec. 1st - 6th. 2nd rounds 18/pr & 900. 4.5 How. were delivered to gun positions. A considerable amount of ammunition was salved and fractions cleared of enemy cars.	
			HONOURS AND REWARDS. 2/Lt. B.W. STIRLING awarded Bar to Military Cross. 9.12.17. for gallantry and devotion to duty nr. the Lille.	
			ADMINISTRATIVE. On 12th. Bde. moved into XIX Corps Reserve Artillery Area, OROMBENE, and remained there until the end of the month.	

R.S. Mellino
Lt. Col. Commanding 15 R.F.A.

14

WAR DIARY
or
INTELLIGENCE SUMMARY

Army Form C. 2118.

18th D.A.C.

Place	Date	Hour	Summary of Events and Information	Remarks and references to Appendices
CROMBEKE	January 1918. 1st.		OFFICERS. The following officers joined from Base during month.	
			Lieut. W.E. Rea. 2/Lt. F.A. Freeman. } 27-1-18	
			2/Lt. A. Shaw. 2/Lt. S. Walcot. 2/Lt. E.Cr. Stephenson	
WAGON LINES 1ST NEAR			and following returned and joining units.	
BOESINGHE 30TH			2/Lt. H. Bottoms 6 52nd Bde. 26-1-18 (attached)	
			2/Lt. E. Emily 2/Lt. J. Stegan 2/Lt. P.H. Young 2/Lt. H.S. Peach. 2/Lt. S. Downing	
			2/Lt. Yeo Best 2/Lt. N. Wilson joined the 6 82nd Bde. 29-1-18.	
			2/Lt. H. Parker — Hospital. 14-1-18.	
			HOSPITAL. 3 Offrs. and 11 Oners. was admitted sick.	
			3 " 3 " was wounded in action and	
			was struck off as follows :- 6 duty 5. evacuated 13.	
			No renewals, I was wounded and remained at duty	
			The officers + O.R's has been very scarce during	
			the month.	

WAR DIARY
or
INTELLIGENCE SUMMARY.

(Erase heading not required.)

Army Form C. 2118.

Place	Date	Hour	Summary of Events and Information	Remarks and references to Appendices
WHBON LINES	1st			
NEAR	to		REINFORCEMENTS.	
BOESINGHE	30th		Reinforcements from Base. 4-Jan-1918. 16th Bn. 5 Gun.	
			" " " " 7 " " 17 Gns. 10 Drivers	
			" " " " 10th " 13 Gun.	
			" " " " 12th " 4 Gns. 3 Drs.	
			" " " " 15th " 1 Wheeler	
			" " " " 23rd " 10 Gunners	
			" " " " 24th " 3 Drivers. 6 Gns. 1 Sh. Sm.	
			Reinforcements were posted to Brigade as under :-	
			To 52nd Bn. 13-1-18. 16 Gunners 2 Drivers	
			" 83rd " 13-1-18. 2 Sergts. 1 Driver	
			" 82nd " 16-1-18. 4 Gns. 3 Drivers	
			" 83rd " 21-1-18. 12 Gns.	
			" 83rd " 21-1-18 5 Gns.	
			1 Sergt. was posted to 83rd Bn. from 82nd Bn. on 29-1-18.	

WAR DIARY
or
INTELLIGENCE SUMMARY.

(Erase heading not required.)

Army Form C. 2118.

Place	Date	Hour	Summary of Events and Information	Remarks and references to Appendices
WAGON LINES NEAR BOESINGHE	1ST TO 30TH		**ANIMALS.** 4 Animals were sent to M.V.S. suffering from mouth and 1 pony was received from Remount Depot CALAIS. on 15-1-18. 19.L.D. on 14-1-18. H. L.D. 1 L.D. returned from M.V.S. on 20-1-18. 1.L.D. from 18.5 R.H.A. on 18-1-18. **AMMUNITION AND SALVAGE.** While in the BOESINGHE area entire column was engaged in Salvage work in the forward area. A scheme was arranged and with the assistance of lorries of M.T. the following amounts of ammunition were salved. The recovered ammunition was dumped near Battery positions for expenditure. The unserviceable and empty cases were delivered to XIX Corps Salvage Dumps. SERVICEABLE 18-pdr:- 24,386 rounds. " 4.5/ons:- 10,240 and 866 Clay 20.	

Army Form C. 2118.

WAR DIARY
or
INTELLIGENCE SUMMARY.
(Erase heading not required.)

Instructions regarding War Diaries and Intelligence Summaries are contained in F. S. Regs., Part II. and the Staff Manual respectively. Title pages will be prepared in manuscript.

Place	Date	Hour	Summary of Events and Information	Remarks and references to Appendices
WAGON LINES NEAR BOESINGHE	13/1. To 30/7/17		UNSERVICEABLE. 18-ph. 61,510 rounds. 4.5" How. S: - 10,392 " 1040 charges. FRENCH "75". 496 rounds. Empty CARTRIDGE CASES. 128 G.S. wagon loads. 163. 4. G.S. " " 16. Railway trucks. In addition to the foregoing 90 G.S. wagon loads of mixed unserviceable were delivered to various dumps of DECAUVILLE TRACK. and 48. G.S. wagon loads of metal unserviceable were delivered to Forward Ammunition Refilling Point. 5. 18 pdr limbers and part of a German 5.9 gun were also collected. As the forward area in which the salvage work was carried out was practically under water the work was rendered extremely difficult.	

Army Form C. 2118.

WAR DIARY
or
INTELLIGENCE SUMMARY.
(Erase heading not required.)

Instructions regarding War Diaries and Intelligence
Summaries are contained in F. S. Regs., Part II.
and the Staff Manual respectively. Title pages
will be prepared in manuscript.

Place	Date	Hour	Summary of Events and Information	Remarks and references to Appendices
WAGON LINES	30th		One sub Div. ordered ecus ready for the unit to take over wagon lines in MAMHOEK area	
NEAR MAMHOEK	31st		Column moved to MAMHOEK AREA on 30th Jan.	

1-2-18.

F.T. Hopkinson Lt Col.
Lieut. Colonel R.F.A.
Commanding 18th Div. Amm. Col.

WAR DIARY
or
INTELLIGENCE SUMMARY.

1 SD Aux Coy
Vol 30

Place	Date	Hour	Summary of Events and Information	Remarks and references to Appendices
HAM HOEK	1st to 10th		AMMUNITION During the month the unit was engaged on work in 1st areas and no ammunition was delivered.	
PONT L'EVEQUE	11th to 15th		ADMINISTRATIVE On the 9th D.R. arrived with orders for the Coy. to transfer to 15th Army. The unit entrained at PROVEN on 10th Feb. and arrived PONT L'EVEQUE on 11th remained in this area for 4 days. Orders were subsequently received for Blanc S. move to GUISCARD on 15th inst. This move was completed	
GUISCARD	15th to 24th		on 15th Feb.	
ROUEZ	28th		On 19th Feb. 15D's Adv. Party went forward to arrange to occupy GATE zone. On the 20th only unit is moved to No 2 Section is move with 3rd Div to forward area on 21st.	

WAR DIARY
or
INTELLIGENCE SUMMARY.

Army Form C. 2118.

(Erase heading not required.)

Instructions regarding War Diaries and Intelligence Summaries are contained in F. S. Regs., Part II. and the Staff Manual respectively. Title pages will be prepared in manuscript.

Place	Date	Hour	Summary of Events and Information	Remarks and references to Appendices
HAM-DEN			Hospital. 4 Gunners and 6 Drivers were admitted sick	
1ST to 10TH			and evacuated. This is a marked decrease on last months figures. Sickness rate as a whole very low.	
PONT L'EVEQUE				
11 to 15TH			Reinforcements. From Base. 3-2-18. 5 Drivers. 28 Gunners.	
			" 11-2-18. 2 Gunners. 2 Drivers.	
			" 16-2-18. 2 Sergeants.	
GUISCARD				
15TH to 24TH			" 27-2-18. 6 Drivers	
			To Brigades. 82nd Bde. 9-2-18. 13 Gunners. 1 Driver	
			83rd " 9-2-18. 22 Gunners.	
ROUEZ			82nd " 18-2-18. 1 Sergt. 2 Gunners.	
28TH			83rd " 18-2-18. 1 Sergt + Gunners.	
			ANIMALS. During the month, 3 R. 2 A.D. - 3 L.D.M. were sent to Mobile Vet Section 1 R. 4 L.D.M. received from M.V.S. on 20-2-18	

Army Form C. 2118.

WAR DIARY
or
INTELLIGENCE SUMMARY.
(Erase heading not required.)

Instructions regarding War Diaries and Intelligence Summaries are contained in F. S. Regs., Part II. and the Staff Manual respectively. Title pages will be prepared in manuscript.

Place	Date	Hour	Summary of Events and Information	Remarks and references to Appendices
HAMHOEK	1-2-18		OFFICERS	
			During the month the following arrivals and departures of Officers occurred.	
1st to 10th			From Base 8-2-18. 2/Lt. J.H. Bradshaw, 2/Lt. R.E. Walker, 2/Lt. M. Powis from Base 8-2-18.	
PONT LEVEQUE			" 13-2-18. 2/Lt. J. Elliot 24-2-18. 2/Lt. S.W. George on first appointment from 179 Battery.	
11th to 13th				
		24-2-18	" 2/Lt. W.G. de Bordoano, 2/Lt. R.M. Paterson, 2/Lt. A. Keith. 2/Lt. L.A. Woods, 2/Lt. G.E. Hampshire, 2/Lt. F. Andrews.	
GUISCARD			Lt. J.A. Apley to join on termination of leave.	
15th to 24th			Potter with effect from 15-2-18.	
ROUEZ		24-2-18	Lt. L.A. Guier, John A/B and B20.	
		4-2-18	2/Lt. L.J. Smith to 83rd Bde, 2/Lt. H. Batham 2-7-83.	
28th		4-2-18	Capt. R.E. Horgan 6 Canad Bde e/c L/F Kingston.	
		on 3-2-18	2/Lt. L.R. Arthur, sick L in DRS 21-2-18.	
			The following two Officers were ordered to England on acct of having obtained their commissions.	
			2/Lt. H. Parker 20-1-18.	
			2/Lt. J.M. Ballard 12-11-17.	

Army Form C. 2118.

WAR DIARY
or
INTELLIGENCE SUMMARY.
(Erase heading not required.)

Instructions regarding War Diaries and Intelligence Summaries are contained in F. S. Regs., Part II. and the Staff Manual respectively. Title pages will be prepared in manuscript.

Place	Date	Hour	Summary of Events and Information	Remarks and references to Appendices
HAMMIDEK	1st 10. 1917.		On 23rd inst. S.M. Section moved to VILLEQUIER AUMONT for work under 58th Div. R.E.	
PONT L'EVEQUE	11th inst.		On 24th L.B. Headquarters & No.1 Section moved to ROUEZ and VILLEQUIER AUMONT respectively	
GUISCARD	15th. 27th		On 28th. 18 Div. Administrative Arrangement for defence and amendment 1 were received. 18 C.R.A. Order No. 13. and amendment 1 received further on reference to Defence were received.	
ROUEZ	28th			

H. Johnston
Lieut. R.E.
Commanding 18 Div. Am. B.C.

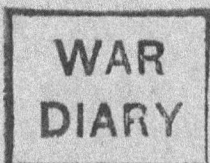

18th DIVISIONAL AMMUNITION COLUMN, R.F.A.

M A R C H

1 9 1 8

Army Form C. 2118.

WAR DIARY
or
INTELLIGENCE SUMMARY.
(Erase heading not required.)

Place	Date	Hour	Summary of Events and Information	Remarks and references to Appendices
ROUEZ	Oct 10	22nd	OFFICERS. The following photographs of officers took place during the month.	
			1st Lieut R.P. Taylor from Base 2nd/Lt R.V. Walker S. Lifely and 2nd/Lieut from Base	
			2nd/Lt H. Andrews & R.S. Walker to The Batteries. 2nd/Lt R.B. Leylands attached 18th Div Brigade	
			2nd 2/Lt R.M. Pattison attached C/93rd Brigade. 2nd/Lt G.E. Hampshire attached A/Zma	
			Brigade. 12th 2nd/Lieut R.V. Martin attached B/82nd Bde. 11th S. Lifely attached	
			82nd Brigade. 15th 2nd/Lt A. E. Curlopp from Base. 18th 2nd/Lt S. Lifely rejoined from	
			92nd Bde. 19th 2nd/Lt A.E. Rudoff joined B/82nd Bde. 24th Lieut S. Mitchell joined	
			Base. 24th 2nd/Lieut O.J. Butler to 82nd Bde. 25th Capt B.W. Hallett (General Services)	
			wounded in action invalided to England.	
			Hospital. Following N.C.Os and men were attended to Hospital with exception	
			of as shown. This is a slight increase on last months figures.	
			1 Corpl. 1 Bdr. 1 Sergt. Sick. 1 Br. Wounded 10 drivers 5 Gunners	
			Damaged Hoofs. 1 Bdr. 1 Wearing coach. 2Gr. 4 drivers Remainder evacuated	
			Reinforcements. Reinforcements were received from Base and posted	
			to Brigades as follows:—	
			1/3/18 from Base 1 Sergt. 1st Horse Base 2 Gr. 2 Corpls. H.Bs. 10 Gr. 10 Dr.	

Army Form C. 2118.

WAR DIARY
or
INTELLIGENCE SUMMARY.
(Erase heading not required.)

Instructions regarding War Diaries and Intelligence Summaries are contained in F.S. Regs., Part II. and the Staff Manual respectively. Title pages will be prepared in manuscript.

[Stamp: ROYAL FIELD ARTILLERY / 18th Div. Ammn. Column / Reg. No. / Date]

Place	Date	Hour	Summary of Events and Information	Remarks and references to Appendices
ROUEZ	1/16 2nd		Reinforcements: From Base 13" 19 Gr 7 Drivers Leg! 18" Yeom Bmb 12 Gr 1 Sgt	
			1" to 82nd Brigade 1 Sgt – 8" to 83rd Brigade 1 Corp! 6 Gr H Drivers	
			9" to 83rd Bde – 1 Fitter 2 Drivers – 11" to 82nd Bde 1 Sergt 2 Corpls 2 Drivers	
			14" to French Mission – 6 Gunners – 15" to 82nd Bde 6 Gunners 5 Drivers to 73rd Bde	
			15" to French Mission – 6 Gunners –	
			Evacuated 28" 7.10 LD were evacuated being too unfit	
ROUEZ	20"		GENERAL REMARKS Orders were received from IX Corps to attack east of Moislains "Moislains" position. Our attack in 1st Front consisted of advancing from 700 to VILLEQUIER-AUMONT on 22nd Bn. and eastern wire second on Holnon area to VILLEQUIER-AUMONT. On 22nd Bn.	
VILLEQUIER-AUMONT 22nd			moved to BOIS de CAUMONT area. On 23rd HQ No 1 column moved to BETHANCOURT sect No 2 + 3	
BOIS DE CAUMONT 22nd			column to GRANDRU. 4B + No 1 section moved on 24" to PORQUERICOURT VR PAROUEF – No 3	
BETHANCOURT 23rd			Section to GRANDRU.	
GRANDRU			Section moved to PONT L'EVEQUE – No 2 section moved to CAISNES area under the orders of 83rd	
PORQUERICOURT PONT L'EVEQUE 24th			Brigade. On 25" HQ 9 No 1 section moved to RIBECOURT and 3 column from PONT L'EVEQUE	
RIBECOURT CAISNES 25th			to PONTOISE – On 26" 4B + No 1 section moved to THUROTTE and No 2 section to NAMPEL	
PONTOISE THUROTTE CAISNES NAMPCEL 26"			On 27" HQ No 1 sect. No 2 section moved to HAUTE-BRAVE via NAMPEL.	
HAUTE BRAVE 27"			Rain fell 3rd column marched to LONGUEIL ST MARIE – No 2 column moved to	
			TRACY-LE MONT	

Army Form C. 2118.

WAR DIARY
or
INTELLIGENCE SUMMARY.
(Erase heading not required.)

Instructions regarding War Diaries and Intelligence Summaries are contained in F. S. Regs., Part II. and the Staff Manual respectively. Title pages will be prepared in manuscript.

Place	Date	Hour	Summary of Events and Information	Remarks and references to Appendices
LONGUEIL-ST MARIE area	31st			
LIANCOURT AREA	1st		On the 31st Column moved to LIANCOURT AREA. During the whole period of the withdrawal the B.A.C were continuously sending ammunition to the gun positions &/or firing batteries. Keeping in close touch with the batteries they supplied Brigades. On one occasion the teams and limbers of No 2 Battery whilst delivering ammunition were called upon to withdraw the guns of 402 Batt. and 2 Batt R.F.A. which were in action. They were very successfully accomplished saving the guns and were enabled them to be used to fight a rearguard action. Communication between Headquarters 18 RFA & Brigades were maintained during the whole withdrawal.	

F. Johnston Lieut Col R.F.A.
Commanding 18th Div Ammn Col

18th DIVISIONAL AMMUNITION COLUMN.

A P R I L

1 9 1 8

WAR DIARY or INTELLIGENCE SUMMARY

Army Form C. 2118.

190 Am Col   WT 32

Place	Date	Hour	Summary of Events and Information	Remarks and references to Appendices
LIANCOURT AREA	1.4.18		**OFFICERS** Arrivals and departures of Officers during the month were as follows:-	
ST RIMAULT	2.4.18		POSTINGS FROM BASE. 12.4.18. 2/Lt G.G. SIMPSON	
VIEFVILLERS	3.4.18		12.4.18. T.N. JENNINGS — H.C. BARNES — F.H. GOODWIN — W.H. CASSELLS	
FRESNOY-AU-VAL	4.4.18		13.4.18. Lt A.H. BASFORD — 2/Lt W. SCORER	
BUSSY-LE-POIX	5.4.18		21.4.18. 2/Lt G.W. DIXON	
			20.4.18. Lt F.A. SIMONDS. U.S.M.O.R.C. from 55" Field Ambulance.	
CHARNY	8.4.18		FROM 82nd BRIGADE. 9.4.18. Major J.D. CROCKER.	
WARLUS	10.4.18		FROM 83rd BRIGADE. 6.4.18. Lt S. LENNIE	
GRANDSART	11.4.18		16.4.18. 2/Lt L.A. WOODS.	
RIVERY (AMIENS)	15.4.18		EVACUATION 15.4.18. Lt I.I. PARSONS. U.S.M.O.R.C. Wounded.	
BOVES	16.4.18		POSTINGS TO BRIGADES. 9.4.18. LIEUT. F.H.T ATKEY to 83rd Brigade. 2/LIEUT. L. ORCHARD to 83rd Bde.	
ST. OUEN	29.4.18		16.4.18. 2/LIEUT. F.H. GOODWIN to 83rd Bde.	
			HOSPITAL. Admissions to Hospital were as follows. 8. Gunners 5 Drivers	
			1 Bombardier. 1 Gunner & 2 Drivers were returned to duty. The remainder were evacuated, a slight decrease on last months figures.	
			REINFORCEMENTS FROM BASE DEPOT. 13.4.18. 1 Sergeant. 16 Drivers	
			TO BRIGADES. To 83rd Bde. 9.4.18. 1 Driver.	
				11.4.18. 1 Sergeant. 1 Bom:r
				12.4.18. 1 Bombardier
				21.4.18. 1 Gunner.

Army Form C. 2118.

WAR DIARY
or
INTELLIGENCE SUMMARY.
(Erase heading not required.)

Place	Date	Hour	Summary of Events and Information	Remarks and references to Appendices
			Arrivals:— 2 R.Dns. and 12 L.D. arrivals were evacuated to M.V.S. during the month. 56 L.D. received for D.A.D. on 12.4.18.	
			General Remarks. On the 2nd inst the D.A.C. moved from the LIANCOURT AREA and by long daily marches via ST RIMAULT — VIEFVILLERS — FRESSNOY AU VAL — BUSSY-LE-POIX — CHARNY — and HAREAS were brought into the Fourth Army collecting area GRANDSART where they remained for four days to be re-equipped. On the 15th inst the Column moved to RIVERY (AMIENS) for the night and on the 16th moved into the line in the BOVES area on the VILLERS-BRETONEUX Sector where in the area that one 2 section were temporarily attached to the 583 Divisional Artillery. On the 58th Div Arty leaving the area both sections were employed in clearing various gun positions of supplies. A large amount of salvage effects and a large amount of salvage effects generally	

Army Form C. 2118.

WAR DIARY
or
INTELLIGENCE SUMMARY.
(Erase heading not required.)

Instructions regarding War Diaries and Intelligence Summaries are contained in F. S. Regs., Part II and the Staff Manual respectively. Title pages will be prepared in manuscript.

Place	Date	Hour	Summary of Events and Information	Remarks and references to Appendices
			On the 28th instr. orders were received for 18th Divisional A.C. to move into the BETHENCOURT — ST. OUEN area and the move was carried out on the 29th April.	

J C Johnston
Lieut. Colonel. R.F.A.
Comdg 18th Div. Ammn Column.

A5834 Wt. W4973/M687 750,000 8/16 D. D. & L. Ltd. Forms/C.2118/13.

WAR DIARY
or
INTELLIGENCE SUMMARY.
(Erase heading not required.)

Army Form C. 2118.

HEADQUARTERS,
18th DIVISIONAL
AMMUNITION COLUMN.

No. M.I.C.I.
Date 1.5.18

Vol 33

Place	Date	Hour	Summary of Events and Information	Remarks and references to Appendices
ST QUEN	1-5-18 to 3-5-18		Officers. 2/Lt A.D. Irving 2/Lt M.L. Harris From Base 13.5.18	
BEHENCOURT	3-5-18 to 31-5-18		2/Lt S.D. Cooper From Base 25-5-18 2/Lt James Neill From Base 31-5-18	
			Lieut L.V. Ormond From Base 29-5-18	
			2/Lt J. McPherson from 282nd Brigade 1-5-18	
			2/Lt H.C. Barnes Posted to C/83rd Brigade 2.5.18	
			Major J.C. Crocker and Lieut Kerins admitted Hospital 4.5.18	
			2/Lt W.C. Chapell Attached B/82nd Brigade 9.5.18. Subsequently posted	
			Lieut R.P. Finnis MC Posted to 96" HAC Brigade Amm Col. 9.5.18	
			Lieut J.H.O. Grier To duty from Hospital 28.4.18	
			2/Lt A. McCowe Posted Y/18 Med. Trh Battery	
			Capt. A. Lyttle Admitted Hospital 14.5.18	
			Capt W.H. Moose to BAC on 18.5.18 to take temporary command	
			of L.F.A. Section vice Capt A. Lyttle to Hospital.	
			2/Lieut Y.H. Holyoak To 82nd Brigade as acting adjutant vice	
			Capt Moore with effect from 18.5.18	
			2/Lieut W. Winter Posted D/82nd Brigade 26.5.18	
			2/Lieut M.L. Harris Posted B/83rd Brigade 20.5.18	
			2/Lieut L. Lapsley to England to receive medical opinion 30.5.18	
			2/Lieut A.D. Irving to 82nd Brigade 30.5.18	
			2/Lt S.D. Cooper & Lieut W.C. de Berdiana to E/18 H.M. Battery 28.5.18	
			2/Lieut M. Serr. Wounded at Front and admitted Hospital 31.5.18	

Army Form C. 2118.

HEADQUARTERS,
16th DIVISIONAL
AMMUNITION COLUMN.

No ....
Date ....

WAR DIARY
or
INTELLIGENCE SUMMARY.
(Erase heading not required.)

Instructions regarding War Diaries and Intelligence Summaries are contained in F. S. Regs., Part II and the Staff Manual respectively. Title pages will be prepared in manuscript.

Place	Date	Hour	Summary of Events and Information	Remarks and references to Appendices
ST OUEN	1-5-18 to 3-5-18		REINFORCEMENTS: The following reinforcements were received during the month	
	14.5.18		1 Driver from B/246 Bde. RFA	
BEHENCOURT	5-5-18 to 31-5-18	16.5.18	1 Corpl. (Bomb) 1 Fitter 40 Gunners 14 Drivers received from Base through Fourth Army collecting area	
			These were distributed as follows:—	
			H.Q.R.Q. 16" Div. 1 Gunner	
			13rd Brigade RFA 1 Corpl. 1 Bomb. 1 Fitter 15 Gunners 7 Drivers	
			16" R.A Trench Mortar Batts. 15 Gunners	
			D.A.C. 10 Gunners 7 Drivers	
		23.5.18	1 Bomb. from C/83rd Brigade	
		24.5.18	1 Bomb. 12 Gunners 3 Drivers from Base through Fourth Army collecting area	
			Postings to Brigades	
		24.5.18	3 Gunners & 2 Drivers to 82nd Brigade	
		" "	1 Bombardier and 6 Gunners to 83rd Brigade	
		" "	3 Gunners to 16" R.A French Mortar Batteries	
		30.5.18	1 Driver to 83rd Brigade	

Army Form C. 2118.

HEADQUARTERS,
13th DIVISIONAL
AMMUNITION COLUMN.

	Remarks and references to Appendices
No. H1/6/1	
Date 2/6/18.	

WAR DIARY
or
INTELLIGENCE SUMMARY.
(Erase heading not required.)

Instructions regarding War Diaries and Intelligence Summaries are contained in F. S. Regs., Part II. and the Staff Manual respectively. Title pages will be prepared in manuscript.

Place	Date	Hour	Summary of Events and Information
ST OUEN.	7.5.18 to 3.5.18.		**Animals.** 2 Riding 13 Light draught Horses and 10 mules were struck off strength during the month evacuated to Mobile Veterinary Section. 1 Riding Horse was destroyed. 8 L.D. were received H 5.18.
BEHENCOURT	3.5.18 to 31.5.18.		**Hospital.** 1 S. Smith 1 Corpl. 8 Drivers admitted to hospital during month. 1 Corpl. 1 Driver discharged to duty.
			Administrative and Generally. On the 2nd inst 18" D.A. warning order was received and on the 3rd inst DAC marched to BEHENCOURT to relieve 2nd Australian DAC. This relief however was not carried out until 4th May. On the 4" 18" DA Orders No. 22. 3. H were received. On relief 2nd Australian DAC handed over Corps Defence Scheme.

A5834 Wt W4973/M687 750,000 8/16 D. D. & L. Ltd. Forms/C.2118/13.

Army Form C. 2118.

HEADQUARTERS,
18th DIVISIONAL
AMMUNITION COLUMN.

No. A/4/7
Date 7.16.18

WAR DIARY
or
INTELLIGENCE SUMMARY.
(Erase heading not required.)

Place	Date	Hour	Summary of Events and Information	Remarks and references to Appendices
ST OUEN	1-5.18		On 9th May 18 DA Order No 25 & I.O.S Calls were received.	
	6.5.18		18 DAD manoeuvres No 2b relative to programme of increasing	
	3.5.18		fire received on the 10th	
BEHENCOURT	3.5.18		On the 16th Relief programme	
			of batteries received and operation order No 131 received on 18th May	
	3.6.18		18 DAO No 28 & 29 received on 21st & 23rd May respectively relative	
			to relief of Divisional Artillery.	
			AA return of DAC returns and 18 Div O. for lacked work	
			taken as a whole the month was uneventful	
			although enemy aircraft were very active in the bombing	
			raids nearly every night.	
			Percentage of sickness remains small.	

F E Johnston
Lieut. Colonel. R.F.A.
Comdg 18th Div. Ammn Column

WAR DIARY
or
INTELLIGENCE SUMMARY.

Army Form C. 2118.

1 D Am Col

Vol 34

Place	Date	Hour	Summary of Events and Information	Remarks and references to Appendices
BEAUMONT	1-19 6-15		OFFICERS	
Area of BEAUCOURT	19-6-15 30-6-15		Arrivals & departures of officers during June as follows:	
			1/Lt R.H. LIDDELL posted from Base 6/6/15	
			1/Lt R.E. HAM " " 9/6/15	
			2/Lt J. ALDERSON " " 13/6/15	
			2/Lt R.B. BARCLAY " " 13/6/15	
			1/Lt D. LEADBETTER " " 21/6/15	
			2/Lt J. MACMILLAN " " 27/6/15	
			2/Lt A.M. MARSH " " 27/6/15	
			Lt. V. MOSS. attached Fourth Army A.A. Defences 7/6/15	
			1/Lt J. ALDERSON Posted to 9/53 Bde 15/6/15	
			1/Lt S.J. ORMOND attached 52 Bde 4/6/15	
			2/Lt R.B. BARCLAY attached A/53 Bde 15/6/15	
			2/Lt R.H. LIDDELL attached D/53 Bde 27/6/15	
			2/Lt L.A. WOODS. returned from Fourth Army Sig School 27/6/15	for course Repeated DAC 27/6/15
			2/Lt G.W. DIXON rejoined DAC from 15/53 21/6/15	
			1/Lt R.E. HAM admitted to Hospital (sick) 27/6/15	
			2/Lt D.R.V. SHILTON posted to DAC 19/6/15 for duty as 3rd Corps Ammn. Sub Officer	
			1/Lt J. HACK attached to D/52 Bde R.F.A 27/6/15	
			S.D. Cashier to Hospital (wounded) 29/6/15	

Army Form C. 2118.

HEADQUARTERS,
18th DIVISIONAL
AMMUNITION COLUMN.

WAR DIARY
or
INTELLIGENCE SUMMARY.
(Erase heading not required.)

Instructions regarding War Diaries and Intelligence
Summaries are contained in F. S. Regs., Part II
and the Staff Manual respectively. Title pages
will be prepared in manuscript.

Place	Date	Hour	Summary of Events and Information	Remarks and references to Appendices
BETHENCOURT	1-6-18 19.6.18			
BEACOURT AREA	N-6-18 21.6.18		REINFORCEMENTS.	
			The following reinforcements were received during the month:	
	2.6.18		1 Gunner to 83 Bde.	
	13.6.18		1 F.A. 1 Bdr. 21 Gunners & 19 Drivers returned from 153 in.	
	8.6.18		2 Bdr. & 30 Gunners received from Base.	
	26.6.18		11 Gunners posted from Base.	
			The following were posted to Batteries from D.A.C:-	
	6.6.18		1 Gunner to 82 Bde R.F.A.	
	8.6.18		1 Dr/m to 83 Bde R.F.A.	
	10.6.18		1 Dr. to 168 Bde. R.F.A.	
	15.6.18		8 Gunners to 8 Drivers to 82 Bde R.F.A.	
	17.6.18		9 Drivers to 82 Bde R.F.A.	
	20.6.18		13 Gunners to 82 Bde R.F.A.	
	17.6.18		16 Drivers sent to Fourth Army Reinforcement Camp.	
	18.6.18		1 Sergt. to Schools of Instruction.	
	15.6.18		1 Corpl & 3 Gunners & 2 Drivers to 83 Bde R.F.A.	
	21.6.18		1 Bdr. & 7 Gunners to 83 Bde R.F.A.	
	14.6.18		18 Gunners to R.A. T.M. Batteries.	
	20.6.18		7 Gunners & 9 Drivers to R.A. T.M. Batteries.	
	15.6.18		2 Gunners to R.A. T.M. Batteries.	

Army Form C. 2118.

WAR DIARY
or
INTELLIGENCE SUMMARY.

(Erase heading not required.)

Instructions regarding War Diaries and Intelligence Summaries are contained in F. S. Regs., Part II and the Staff Manual respectively. Title pages will be prepared in manuscript.

Place	Date	Hour	Summary of Events and Information	Remarks and references to Appendices
BEAUCOURT	1-6-16		REINFORCEMENTS (CONT'D)	
	29-6-16		21-6-16 4 Gunners posted from 153rd Bde RFA to R.H. T.M.B.	
			+ 3 Gunners from R.H. T.M.B. to 93 Bde RFA	
BEAUCOURT AREA	19-6-16 30-6-16		ANIMALS. 61 animals went struck off the strength during the month & none exposed of as follows:-	
			29 to 22 Bde	
			22 to 93 Bde	
			4 to M.V.S.	
			3 Destroyed by Enemy Shell fire	
			3 Destroyed by V.O. officer	
			――	
			61	
			Casualties 2 Bdr., 2 S.S. 3 Gunners & 9 Drivers admitted to hospital during the month. 1 Bdr., 1 Gunner & 3 Drivers returned from hospital to duty.	
			Ammunition Generally. During this period the D.A.C. delivered a large amount of ammunition to Batteries in the section lines much hard work was carried out revetting & traversing the horse lines to the height of 5 feet. Casualties from shells elsewhere	

WAR DIARY
or
INTELLIGENCE SUMMARY.

Army Form C. 2118.

Place	Date	Hour	Summary of Events and Information	Remarks and references to Appendices
BEHENCOURT	1-6-17 9.6.17		Some featureless light shelling this month. Seeing the latter half of the month, much activity was caused by Gunner fire — as many as 80 men on a section have been out at the same time — but with a few days rest the army recovered.	
BEAUCOURT AREA	9-6-17 30.6.17		On the 19th June the D.A.C. moved from BEHENCOURT village to upon N & E of BEAUCOURT. Very satisfactory was found of grazing & green fodder & all the animals are in excellent condition	

R S Allen Capt
Lieut. Colonel. R.F.A.
Comdg 18th Div. Ammn Column.

Army Form C. 2118.

18D Am Col
Vol 35

WAR DIARY
or
INTELLIGENCE SUMMARY.
(Erase heading not required.)

Instructions regarding War Diaries and Intelligence Summaries are contained in F.S. Regs. Part II. and the Staff Manual respectively. Title pages will be prepared in manuscript.

Place	Date	Hour	Summary of Events and Information	Remarks and references to Appendices
BEAUCOURT AREA. LONGPRÉ-LES-AMIENS	1-7-18 to 14-4-18 3-4-18		OFFICERS. Lieut Lewis D. joined from week leave 3.4.18 — 2/Lt J. macmillan attached D/130 Brigade R.F.A. 3-4-18 — 2/Lt J. Steele attached D/Bn. Brigade 29-6-18 — 2/Lt J. Levine attached to Fourth Army 1st of Defence for course of instruction 8-4-18 — 2/Lt B. Liddelow attached 82nd Brigade R.F.A. 8.4.18 — Lt W.G. de Bertodano Posted from X/18 TM Battery 23.4.18 — Revd W.L. Young — From Base 21.4.18.	
			REINFORCEMENTS. following re-enforcement, joining received were dispatched.	
			From Base 3.4.18 — 130 Gunners 3 Gunners	
			—"— 6.4.18 — 1 Gunner	
			—"— 10.4.18 — 1 Sergeant, 1 Bombardier, 8 Gunners	
			—"— 15.4.18 — 8 Sergeants, 4 Corporals, 1 Gunner	
			From A/290 Bde. 16.4.18 — 2 Gunners	
			From Base. 23.4.18 — 1 Gunner, 11 Drivers	
			To 82nd Brigade 16.4.18 — 2 Sergeants	
			—"— 24.4.18 — 2 Gunners	
			—"— 29.4.18 — 1 Soldier	
			To 83rd Brigade 6.4.18 — 1 Bombardier	
			—"— 16.4.18 — 6 Sergeants, 4 Corporals	
			—"— 25.4.18 — 3 Gunners, 1 Driver	

Army Form C. 2118.

WAR DIARY
or
INTELLIGENCE SUMMARY.
(Erase heading not required.)

Instructions regarding War Diaries and Intelligence Summaries are contained in F. S. Regs., Part II. and the Staff Manual respectively. Title pages will be prepared in manuscript.

Place	Date	Hour	Summary of Events and Information	Remarks and references to Appendices
BEAUCOURT AREA	1-7-18 to 14-7-18		Hospital. 1 Sgt. 1 Corpl. 1 Dr. 1 S/S 18 Btry. and three gunners were admitted. Discharged 15 Btr 1 Corpl. Evacuated 1 Dr. 3 Gunners 3 Drivers 1 S/S Remaining in Hospital 1 S/S	
LONGPRÉ-LES-AMIENS	14-7-18 to 31-7-18		ANIMALS. 10 LD animals evacuated to M.V.S. 31 LD animals received as remounts during month —	
			Administrative Generally. At the beginning of the month the Bde was encamped in the BEAUCOURT area and was relieved by the 44th Divl Arty on the 14th July, was 18 Divl Arty now No 35 at 10.7.18. It was a fairly uneventful period although horses were fully employed with ammunition delivery owing to the shortage of men armed by the officered Army.	

Army Form C. 2118.

WAR DIARY
or
INTELLIGENCE SUMMARY.
(Erase heading not required.)

Place	Date	Hour	Summary of Events and Information	Remarks and references to Appendices
BEAUCOURT 14-14-4-16 LONGPRE-LES-AMIENS.			No. 3 (S.A.A.) Section remained at MONTIGNY under 18" Div. B. to work frontwards. Rest of Div. On the 14" July the D.A.C. moved into the G.H.Q. Reserve area (H.Q. and Nos. 1 & 2 Sections at LONGPRÉ and S.A.S. Section at BREHAN.) Special instructions were issued as to procedure in the event of a move by train. The Division to be prepared to move at nine hours notice (various tables and amendments received). During the period the Div. was at rest, horse shows etc, were arranged and successfully carried out. The leave allotment continues to be restricted and men proceed on leave who have been in the country 15 months and over without leave. The period for Officers leave was increased to seven months —	On

Army Form C. 2118.

WAR DIARY
or
INTELLIGENCE SUMMARY.
(Erase heading not required.)

Place	Date	Hour	Summary of Events and Information	Remarks and references to Appendices
BEAUCOURT AREA 1-14-7-18			On the 28th inst orders as to relief of 5th Australian Bde by 18th AIB were received, relief to take place on or about 1st August.	
HONGPRÉ-LÈS AMIENS 14-31-7-18				

F. Johnston
Lieut & ot DAA
Commanding 18th Aus Annn Bde

8 August 1918.

18th DIVISION.
ARTILLERY.

18th DIVISIONAL AMMUNITION COLUMN   R. F. A.

AUGUST   1918

WAR DIARY
or
INTELLIGENCE SUMMARY.
(Erase heading not required.)

Army Form C. 2118.

18 D Am Col
957 36

Place	Date	Hour	Summary of Events and Information	Remarks and references to Appendices
LONGPRE-LES AMIENS	1-2/8/18		OFFICERS	
FRECHENCOURT	2/8/18		The following casualties affecting Officers occurred during the month.	
			LIEUT. J.F.A. QUIN attached "X" Anti-aircraft Battery for instruction 1-8-18	
	5/8/18 to		2/LIEUT. A.W. MARSH attached 83rd Brigade 5.8.18	
HEILLY	10/4/18		LIEUT. J.F. DOVEY attached 83rd Brigade 6.8.18. Subsequently wounded and evacuated to England 11.8.18.	
ALBERT AREA	23/8/18		2/LIEUT. T.H. HOLYOAK. Posted 92nd Brigade with effect from 18.5.18. Previously attached	
FRICOURT AREA	16-31-8-18		2/LIEUT. L.A. WOODS attached 83rd Brigade 8.8.18 Rejoined 11.8.18	
			2/LIEUT. E. ATKINS " " Rejoined 22.8.18	
			LIEUT. B.W. STIRLING. Admitted hospital sick 6.8.18	
			2/LIEUT. L.A. WOODS attached Fourth Army T.M. School 15.8.18.	
			LIEUT. S. LENNIE. Posted R. Anti-aircraft Battery with effect from 8.7.18.	
			LIEUT. W.C. de Bertodano To Base on medical grounds 8.7.18	
			2/LIEUT. J. YOUNG. Posted from Base 14.8.18 Attached 8/83 Bde 24-8-18	
			LIEUT. A.H. BASFORD " To England sick 11.8.18.	
			2/LIEUT. J.R. OATES. ⎫	
			2/LIEUT. D.M. BERTRAM ⎬ From Base 22.8.18 Attached 83rd Bde 24.8.18.	
			2/LIEUT. T. McN. LAMB ⎭	
			2/LIEUT. A.P. HIBBERD ⎫ From Base 24.8.18.	
			2/LIEUT. W.D. MEREDITH ⎬	
			2/LIEUT. A.F. KIDGELEY ⎭	
			2/LIEUT. C.O. KITCHENER From Base 31.8.18.	
			2/LIEUT. R.H.R. LIDDELL Posted 83rd Bde effect from 20.6.18.	
			2/LIEUT. D.M. BERTRAM Posted 83rd Bde effect from 24.8.18.	

Army Form C. 2118.

WAR DIARY
or
INTELLIGENCE SUMMARY.
(Erase heading not required.)

Place	Date	Hour	Summary of Events and Information	Remarks and references to Appendices
LONGPRÉ-LES-AMIENS	1-2/8/18		REINFORCEMENTS Re-inforcements were received and despatched to Brigades as follows:-	
FRECHENCOURT	2-8-18 to 15/8/18		From Base. 1 Sergeant. 2 Corporals 14 Gunners 1 Driver	
	2.8.18		2 Corporals 8 Bombardiers	
	7.8.18		2 Bombardiers 27 Gunners 10 Drivers	
	10.8.18		8 Gunners 2 Drivers	
HEILLY	16/8/18 to			
	14.8.18		1 Fitter	
	18.8.18		1 Sergeant 1 Corporal	
	22.8.18		1 Sergeant 1 Corporal 1 Bombardier 20 Gunners 3 Drivers	
ALBERT AREA	23-8-18			
	4.8.18		To 82nd Brigade. 3 Drivers	
	20.8.18		" 8 Gunners	
FRICOURT AREA	31-8-18		2.8.18	To 83rd Brigade. 1 Sergt. 2 Drivers	
	8.8.18		" 20 Gunners	
	13.8.18		" 2 Corporals 2 Bomrs 30 Gunners 12 Drivers	
	14.8.18		" 1 Corporal 6 Bombrs	
	25.8.18		" 1 Sergeant 1 Corporal 1 Bombr 12 Gs 3 Drivers	
			ANIMALS	
			6 L.D.H. + 5 Mules evacuated to M.V.S.	
			4 L.D.H. + 2 Mules killed by shell fire.	

— OVER —

Army Form C. 2118.

WAR DIARY
or
INTELLIGENCE SUMMARY.
(Erase heading not required.)

Instructions regarding War Diaries and Intelligence Summaries are contained in F. S. Regs., Part II. and the Staff Manual respectively. Title pages will be prepared in manuscript.

Place	Date	Hour	Summary of Events and Information	Remarks and references to Appendices
			HOSPITAL and PERSONNEL CASUALTIES	
LONGPRE-LES-AMIENS	1-2/8/18		1 Driver killed in action	
FRECHENCOURT	2/8/18		2 Sergeants and 2 Drivers wounded in action	
	6.		6 Drivers to hospital sick (wounded)	
	15/8/18		1 S/S and 1 Saddler to hospital sick. 1/S returned to duty.	
HEILLY	16/8/18			
	16.		Administrative and Generally.	
ALBERT AREA	27-8-18		At the beginning of the month the D.A.C. were at LONGPRÉ-LES-AMIENS in the rest area. Orders having been received to relieve the 5" Australian D.A.C. the Column moved to lines in FRECHENCOURT area on the 2nd inst.	
FRICOURT AREA	28-8-18			
	16		Ammunition supply started on the 3rd inst. and was never varied to get as much forward as possible by the night of the 3rd/4th.	
	31/8/18		On the 8" inst the Division attacked and advanced and from that date to the end of the month Nos 1 and 2 Sections practically became B.A.C.'s to the 2nd and 3rd Brigades for moving warfare operations.	

Army Form C. 2118.

WAR DIARY
or
INTELLIGENCE SUMMARY.
(Erase heading not required.)

Instructions regarding War Diaries and Intelligence Summaries are contained in F.S. Regs., Part II. and the Staff Manual respectively. Title pages will be prepared in manuscript.

Place	Date	Hour	Summary of Events and Information	Remarks and references to Appendices
LUNAPRE-LES AMIENS	1-2/8/18		The 82nd Brigade and No 1 Section were attached to 47" D.A. for tactical work and No 2 Section to the 25" DA.	
FRECHENCOURT	2.8.18 to 15.8.18		The L.A.A Section remain under control of 18' Div R. Orders were issued on the 10" inst to clear all rear positions of Brigade, of ammunition and a great deal of	
HEILLY	16.8.18 to 27.8.18		hard work was necessary to accomplish this. It was however completed, and, in addition, rear positions of the	
ALBERT area	23-8-18		195 Brigade RFA were cleared. A central dump was made at MERICOURT-L'ABBE for all ammunition not required at forward positions.	
FRICOURT area	16.31.8.18		Approximately 45,000 rounds 18 pr and 8000 rds H.5" ammunition was delivered to gun positions during month and approximately 14,000 18 pr and 1000 rds H.5" were salved and delivered to dumps. Notwithstanding the amounts of ammunition to be	

Army Form C. 2118.

WAR DIARY
or
INTELLIGENCE SUMMARY.
(Erase heading not required.)

Place	Date	Hour	Summary of Events and Information	Remarks and references to Appendices
			dealt with, both sections were at the same time carrying out a fatigue of 4 G.S. wagons each daily to cart stone for road repairs to BEAUCOURT from CONTAY. Numerous other small details were carried out during the month. The work accomplished during the month was considerable, and in view of the fact that the Artillery of the Division was engaged in moving warfare it was necessarily somewhat difficult at times to carry out work detailed.	

L E Johnson
Lieut Col R.F.A.
Commanding 19 Divl Ammunition Col.

Headquarters
18 Div Arty

Officer i/c
R.H. & R.F.A. Records

Hereworth War Diary for
September.

13-10-18

[signature]
Lieut Col R.F.A
Commdg — 18 DAC

WAR DIARY
or
INTELLIGENCE SUMMARY.
(Erase heading not required.)

Army Form C. 2118.

Place	Date 1916	Hour	Summary of Events and Information	Remarks and references to Appendices
FRICOURT AREA	August 1st, 2nd		Casualties affecting Officers.	
TRONES WOOD	2nd & 3rd		The followings are the arrivals and departures of officers during the month of September.	
MAUREPAS	3rd-16th		2/Lt A.P. HIBBERD Attached D/82nd Brigade 1-9-16	
MOISLAINS	16th-30th		2/Lt W.D. MEREDITH Attached A/83rd -"- 3.9.16	
			2/Lt A.E. KIDGELEY Attached C/83rd -"- 6.9.16	
			2/Lt H.S. MOSS } From Base. 11.9.18	
			2/Lt T.E. PHEYSEY }	
			2/Lt J.E. PHEYSEY Attached 82nd Brigade	
			2/Lt W.D. MEREDITH Returned from A/83 Bde. 15.9.16.	
			2/Lt H.S. MOSS. Posted 83rd Brigade 14.9.16	
			2/Lt H.T. MOORE. From Base 21-9-16	
			2/Lt H.T. MOORE Posted D/82nd Brigade 22.9.16.	
			2/Lt J.McA. Aitken Posted from Base 26.9.16.	
			2/Lt J.McA. Aitken Attached 82nd Brigade 26.9.16.	
			2/Lt R.E. HART. From Base 28.9.16	
			REINFORCEMENTS	
			Reinforcements were received from Base and posted to Batteries as follows:-	

Army Form C. 2118.

WAR DIARY
or
INTELLIGENCE SUMMARY.
(Erase heading not required.)

18th MGC
Vol 38
Nov Sept.

Place	Date	Hour	Summary of Events and Information	Remarks and references to Appendices
FRICOURT AREA	August 1918			
TRONES WOOD	1st–2nd	2nd–3rd		
MAUREPAS	3rd–16			
MOISLAINS	16–30		Casualties affecting Officers.	

The followings are the arrivals and departures of Officers during the month of September.

2/Lt A. P. HIBBERD   Attached D/82nd Brigade   1-9-18
2/Lt W. D. MEREDITH   Attached A/93rd   3-9-18
2/Lt A. E. MIDGELEY   Attached C/93rd   6-9-18
2/Lt H. S. MOSS   } From Base 11-9-18
2/Lt J. E. PHEYSEY   }
2/Lt J. E. PHEYSEY   Attached 82nd Brigade
2/Lt W. D. MEREDITH   Returned from A/93 Bde.   15-9-18
2/Lt H. S. MOSS   Posted 93rd Brigade   14-9-18
2/Lt H. T. MOORE   From Base   21-9-18
2/Lt H. T. MOORE   Posted D/82nd Brigade   23-9-18
2/Lt J. McAtkin   Posted from Base   26-9-18
2/Lt J. McAtkin   Attached 92nd Brigade   26-9-18
2/Lt R. E. HAM.   From Base   28-9-18

REINFORCEMENTS

Reinforcements were received from Base and posted to Batteries as follows:-

Army Form C. 2118.

WAR DIARY
or
INTELLIGENCE SUMMARY.
(Erase heading not required.)

Place	Date Aug. 1918	Hour	Summary of Events and Information	Remarks and references to Appendices
FRICOURT AREA	1st 2nd			
TRONES WOOD	2nd 3rd		From Base: 3 Corporals 6 Signallers	
MAUREPAS	3rd–15th		" 20 Gunners	
MOISLAINS	16th–30th		4.9.18 " 15 Drivers	
			8.9.17 " 2 Bomdrs 5 Gunners	
			13.9.17 " 1 Fitter	
			15.9.18 " 5 Sergeants 2 Corporals 1 Plumber 4 Drivers and reported	
			17.9.18 " 82nd Brigade	
			18.9.18 " 4 Sergeants, 1 Bomdr 5 Drivers 32 Gunners – duel to 83 Bde.	
			20.9.18 " 3 Bom Cr: 49 Gunners 10 Sigs 12 Drivers	
			30.9.18 " 1 Sergeant 2 Corporals 1 Bombardier 20 Drivers 23 Gunners	
			6 Signallers	

To 82nd Brigade
3.9.18. – 1 Bombardier 9 Gunners 1 Driver
6.9.18. – 1 Corporal 1 Bombardier
12.9.18. – 13 Gunners 7 Drivers
15.9.18. – 1 Shoeing Smith
20.9.18. – 2 Corporals 8 Gunners
28.9.18. – 1 Bombardier 4 Signallers 14 Gunners 5 Drivers
29.9.18. – 1 Sergeant 8 Gunners 6 Drivers

To 83rd Brigade
3.9.18. – 4 Signallers 5 Drivers
4.9.18. – 9 Gunners
6.9.18. – 1 Corporal 6 Signallers

Army Form C. 2118.

WAR DIARY
or
INTELLIGENCE SUMMARY.

(Erase heading not required.)

Instructions regarding War Diaries and Intelligence Summaries are contained in F.S. Regs., Part II. and the Staff Manual respectively. Title pages will be prepared in manuscript.

Place	Date	Hour	Summary of Events and Information	Remarks and references to Appendices
FRICOURT AREA	1 – 2nd			
TRONES WOOD	2 – 3rd		Postings to 83rd Bde continued	
MAUREPAS	3 – 16th		3.9.18: 4 Signallers 5 Drivers	
MOISLAINS	16. 30.		4.9.18: 9 Gunners	
			6.9.18: 6 Signallers	
			8.9.18: 1 Corporal, 1 Bombardier	
			12.9.18: 1 Corporal, 6 Drivers	
			20.9.18: 7 Gunners, 10 Gunners 5 Drivers	
			28.9.18: 5 Sergeants, 2 Sgts	
			29.9.18: 1 Corporal, 1 Corporal, 5 Signallers, 12 Gunners, 3 Drivers	

Animals

2.R. 11 L.D. 7 Mules were evacuated to M.V.S during month.
8 L.D. 5 Mules Killed.

Hospital and Personnel casualties

1 Bombardier, 2 Gunners, 5 Drivers admitted to Hospital & subsequently evacuated.

Army Form C. 2118.

WAR DIARY
or
INTELLIGENCE SUMMARY.
(Erase heading not required.)

Place	Date	Hour	Summary of Events and Information	Remarks and references to Appendices
FRICOURT. ALB.M.	2nd Aug 1916		Administrative Generally. In consequence of progress made the Division moved from FRICOURT to TRONES WOOD remaining there one night and moving the following morning (3rd) to MAUREPAS Area. No. 1 and 2 Sections remained practically as B.A.C's to the 82nd and 83rd Brigades respectively and kept in touch with Batteries during frequent moves. A large amount of ammunition was delivered to positions near positions of Batteries cleared, and ammunition delivered forward. On night of 16-17 bombs were dropped on lines of No 1 Section killing 4 horses + 3 mules and wounding 4 horses + 6 mules. No further casualties occurred — The D.A.C. Sections remain under the orders of 18th Div. D. working with the Infantry Brigades to supply of ammunition etc.	
TRONES WOOD	2nd—3rd			
MAUREPAS.	3 — 16.			
MOISLAINS	16 — 30			

F. C. Johnston, Lt.Col. R.F.A.
O.C. 18th D.A.C.

WAR DIARY
or
INTELLIGENCE SUMMARY

Army Form C. 2118.

18D Am Col

Vol 38

Place	Date 1918 Oct	Hour	Summary of Events and Information	Remarks and references to Appendices
MOISLAINS	1-3rd		Officers	
			The following casualties affecting officers occurred during the month:	
HAZECOURT LE 3rd	3-14		2/Lt. H.S. McINTOSH posted from Base 3/10/15 & returned to 83 Bde HqRs.	
			Lt. D.V.R. SHILTON. Struck off strength and sent from 4/10/15 – on transfer	
SAULCOURT	4-7		2/Lt. R.E. HAM. posted to 83 Bde 7/10/15	
			2/Lt. F. HOPKINS posted to 82 Bde 7/10/15	
BONY	7-9th		2/Lt. L.A. WOODS. Transferred on Sep Instructions to Fourth Army T.M. School with effect from 10/6/15.	
ELINCOURT	9-15"		Lt. V.B. JONES. posted from Base 30/10/15	
AVELU	15-21st		2/Lt. S.E. DONEY. posted from Base 30/10/15.	
MAUROIS	21-27"		2/Lt. A.E. HEDGELEY. Killed in action 17/10/15.	
			Lt. V.B. JONES. Posted to 82 Bde. 31/10/15.	
LE CATEAM	27-31st		2/Lt. J.M. AITKEN. Died of wounds 14/10/15.	
			2/Lt. R.B. BARCLAY. Invalided to England 1/5/15.	
			2/Lt. A.W. MARSH. Wounded in action 14/10/15.	
			Lt. L.J. ORMOND. Posted to 82 Bde under orders from 5/6/15	

Army Form C. 2118.

WAR DIARY
or
INTELLIGENCE SUMMARY.
(Erase heading not required.)

Instructions regarding War Diaries and Intelligence Summaries are contained in F. S. Regs., Part II. and the Staff Manual respectively. Title pages will be prepared in manuscript.

Place	Date	Hour	Summary of Events and Information	Remarks and references to Appendices
	1917			
MOISLAINS	1-3rd		REINFORCEMENTS Reinforcements now received from Base posted to Brigades as under :—	
ALLECOURT LE BAS	3-4th		From Base	
			13-10-17 — 2 Cpls, 9 Gunners, 9 Drivers	
SAULCOURT	4-7th		19-10-17 — 2 Sergts, 3 Bmbdrs, 5 Sigs, 11 Gunners, & 17 Drivers.	
BONY	7-9th		29-10-18 — 17 Gunners, 1 Driver.	
ELINCOURT	9-15		To 52 Bde. RFA	
AVELU	15-17th		21-10-18 — 1 Gunner	
			23-10-18 — 1 Bdr, 4 Gunners, 4 Drivers	
MAUROIS	17-27th		3-10-18 — 1 Sergt, 1 Bdr, 4 Sigrs, 22 Gunners, 12 Drivers	
LE CATEAU	27-31st		To 63rd Bde RFA	
			3-10-18 — 2 Cpls, 2 Bdrs, 1 Saddler, 2 Signallers, 1 Gunner, 7 Drivers	
			23-10-18 — 2 Sergts, 5 Sigs, 15 Gunners, 8 Drivers	
			16-10-18 — 14 Gunners.	
			Animals	
			1 R. 8 L.D.H. & 2 O.M. were reported (surrendered) to M.V.S. during the month	
			1 R. 1 L.D. 2 H.D. & 11 M. were killed during the month.	

Army Form C. 2118.

WAR DIARY
or
INTELLIGENCE SUMMARY.
(Erase heading not required.)

Place	Date Hour	Summary of Events and Information	Remarks and references to Appendices
MOISLAINS	Oct. 1-3rd	HOSPITAL & PERSONNEL CASUALTIES.	
AIZECOURT-LE-BAS	3-4th	1 B.S.M., 1 Sergt & 1 Corporal Killed	
		1 4/Str, 1 Saddler, & 3 Gunners wounded	
SAULCOURT	4-7th	2 Sgts, 1 Cpl, 1 Bdr, 3 Gunners, 9 Drivers admitted hospital	
BONY	7-9th	Administration Generally.	
ELINCOURT	9-15th	Owing the extra burden of moving everyone the	
AVELU	15-21st	D.A.C. was very actively engaged in supplying Ammunition	
MAUROIS	21-27th	to forward gun positions and in moving the ART'S forward.	
LE CATEAU	27-31st	Being continually on the move, enforced much hard	
		work on both men & horses — the latter standing	
		the extra work extremely well.	

J. Johnston
Lieut. Colonel R.F.A.
Comdg 18th Div. Ammn Column.

WAR DIARY
or
INTELLIGENCE SUMMARY
(Erase heading not required.)

Army Form C. 2118.

18 D Amm C Vol 39

Place	Date 1918 NOV	Hour	Summary of Events and Information	Remarks and references to Appendices
LE CATEAU	1/11/18 3/11/18		Officers — The following casualties affecting officers occurred during the month	
MARETZ	8/11/18 30/11/18		2/Lt E.S. HARDACRE — posted from Base 1/11/18 & attached to 53 Bde 7/11/15	
			2/Lt H. GLASIER — posted from Base 1/11/18 & attached to DTMB 7/11/18	
			2/Lt R.L. MANBY — posted from Base 7/11/15 & attached to 53 Bde 7/11/15	
			Capt D.J.C. HEARN (C.F.) posted to DAC 17/11/18	
			2/Lt A.P. HIBBERD — posted from Base 19/11/18	
			2/Lt H.A. BROWN — posted from Base 27/11/18	
			2/Lt H.C. CATCHESIDE — posted from Base 27/11/18	
			2/Lt J.F.A. QUIN — Strict Strength — Medical Board sitted by War Office	Auth: 18 Div. 12 296/176 "A".
			REINFORCEMENTS	
			Reinforcements were received from Base posted to Brigades as under:-	
			FROM BASE	
			8-11-18 — 3 Cpls, 4 Bmdrs, 5 Gunners + 3 Drivers	
			15-11-18 — 3 Bmdrs, 7 Gunners + 5 Signallers	
			22-11-18 — 2 Sergts, 5 Cpls, 3 Bmdrs, 15 Gunners	
			30-11-18 — 1 Sergt. 1 Cpl. 33 Gunners, 2 Drivers	

Army Form C. 2118.

WAR DIARY
or
INTELLIGENCE SUMMARY.
(Erase heading not required.)

Place	Date Nov.	Hour	Summary of Events and Information	Remarks and references to Appendices
LE CATEAU	1-11-18 to 8-11-18			
MARETZ	9-11-18 to 30-11-18		Reinforcements (Contd.)	
			To 82 Bde RFA	
			10-11-18 — 1 Corpl + 1 Bomdr.	
			20-11-18 — 2 Btrs, 2 Signallers, 7 Drivers	
			26-11-18 — 2 Sergts, 3 Corpls, 2 Bomdrs + 12 Gunners	
			30-11-18 — 1 Corpl.	
			To 83 Bde RFA	
			2-11-18 — 9 Gunners	
			4-11-18 — 4 Drivers	
			10-11-18 — 1 Corpl, 1 Bomdr.	
			20-11-18 — 1 Bomdr, 4 Drivers	
			26-11-18 — 1 Bomdr.	
			To DTM B	
			11-11-18 — 2 Bomdrs.	
			14-11-18 — 1 Corpl, 2 Bomdrs + 3 Signallers.	
			ANIMALS	
			9 + D.H. + 6 L.D.M. were evacuated (sick) during month to M.V.S.	
			1 R.H. + 3 L.D.M. were destroyed during the month	

Army Form C. 2118.

WAR DIARY
or
INTELLIGENCE SUMMARY.
(Erase heading not required.)

Instructions regarding War Diaries and Intelligence Summaries are contained in F. S. Regs., Part II. and the Staff Manual respectively. Title pages will be prepared in manuscript.

Place	Date Nov	Hour	Summary of Events and Information	Remarks and references to Appendices
LE CATEAU	1-11-18 8-11-18		HOSPITAL & PERSONNEL CASUALTIES 1 Sergt, 1 Bmdr, 1 S/S, 4 Gunners & 3 Drivers admitted to hospital (Sick)	
MARETZ	9-11-18 30-11-18		Administrative General Since the cessation of hostilities the Unit has been actively engaged in supplying rations &c. to forward area, & in daily salvage work in the surrounding districts. Many fatigues have been carried out, including the collection of enemy guns, and conveying same to the various Trophy Parks. At the present time various classes lectures are being held in connection with the educational scheme for demobilization.	

J. Johnston
Lieut. Colonel, R.F.A.
Comdg 18th Div. Ammn Column.

WAR DIARY
or
INTELLIGENCE SUMMARY

(Erase heading not required.)

Army Form C. 2118

18 D Am C./

J.D. 40

Place	Date	Hour	Summary of Events and Information	Remarks and references to Appendices
MARETZ	1-12-18 to 31-12-18		**Officers** The following casualties affecting officers occurred during the month. 2/Lt. E.S. HARDACRE. to England 9/12/1918 - Auth: W.O. letter 2/Evacuations/-14637 R.S.6(A) dt. 27/11/1918. Lt. E.W. NURSE posted to 18th D.A.C. 18/12/1918. **REINFORCEMENTS.** Reinforcements were received from Base & posted to Brigades as under:- **From Base** 9-12-18 — 8 Drivers. 22-12-18 — 37 Gunners. 27-12-18 — 4 Sgt. 5 Cpl. 4 Bdr. 10 Signallers, 41 Gunners. 29-12-18 — 1 Farr S.Sgt. 1 Cpl. 3 Bdrs. 5 Gunners, 1 Driver. **To 82 Bde RFA** 6/12/18 — 2 Sergts. 1 Cpl. 10/12/18 — 1 Bdr. 11 Gunners 24/12/18 — 15 Gunners 30/12/18 — 1 Sergt. 20 Gunners.	

WAR DIARY or INTELLIGENCE SUMMARY

Army Form C. 2118

Place	Date 1918	Hour	Summary of Events and Information	Remarks and references to Appendices
MARETZ	1-12-18 to 31-12-18		Reinforcements (Cont'd) To 83rd Bde R.F.A. 5/12/18 7 Gunners 10/12/18 16 Gunners 23/12/18 15 Gunners 30/12/18 1 Sgt. 2 Cpls, 11 Gunners. 66 O.R. despatched to CAMBRIA (during the month) for demobilisation. ANIMALS 3 L.D.H. + 3 L.D.M. evacuated during the month, to M.V.S. 1 R. + 1 L.D.M. died 3 L.D.M. – LOST. HOSPITAL & PERSONNEL CASUALTIES 1 Col. Sgt., 1 Bdr., 1 Sh., 5 Gunners, & 9 Drivers admitted to hospital during the month. ADMINISTRATIVE & GENERAL During the month this Unit has been actively engaged in salvage work, and in assisting the farmers in the neighbourhood in agricultural work, such as ploughing etc. M. White Capt. 18th Div. Amm. Column.	

Army Form C. 2118.

WAR DIARY
or
INTELLIGENCE SUMMARY.
(Erase heading not required.)

Place	Date	Hour	Summary of Events and Information	Remarks and references to Appendices
MERSA	1/1/19 to 31/1/19		JANUARY 1919.	

ANIMALS. The following horses were evacuated

TO M.V.S.
- 4-1-19.   1 D.
- 16-1-19. 1 R.
- 29-1-19. 1 L.D.
- 30-1-19. 1 L.D.
- 5-1-19.   1 L.D.

DIED.
- 26-1-19. 1 L.D.
- 24-1-19. 1 L.D.

DESTROYED 20-1-19. 1 L.D.

HOSPITAL. The following were admitted to hospital
- 5 GNRS.
- 4 DRIVERS.
- 1 BUNNER (Bronchi pneumonia).

DEATHS.

ADMINISTRATIVE & GENERAL.
During January the unit has been actively employed on the SAUVAGE work in the area & in assisting French farmers in agricultural work.

H. Johnston
Commanding 18 Bty R.F.A.

Army Form C. 2118.

18 D. Amn Coy

WAR DIARY
or
INTELLIGENCE SUMMARY.

(Erase heading not required.)

March, 1919.

Place	Date	Hour	Summary of Events and Information	Remarks and references to Appendices
Havre	1/3/19		The following Personnel were posted to 67 Coy. on arrival:	
	6-3-19		1 Cpl. 3 Bars. 1 C.S.M. 3 H.Dvrs. 1 C.S.M. 3 P.S. 39 G.W. 39 Dr.	
	12-3-19		1 H.Dvr. 1 Sadler. 2 Sigmllrs. 1 G.T.	
	To-10th Bar. 23-3-19		" Do. "	
	15/3/19		Reinforcements. During the month reinforcements for Divisions	
			were received as follows:	
	6-3-19	7	5-3-19. 7.	
	7-3-19	11	16-3-19. 7.	
Montigny	12-3-19	465	20-3-19. 7.	
			24-3-19. 1.	
	15/3/19		INDIANS. During the month 7 G. & Dr.	
			2 Sams.	
	31/3/19		General. On the 15th of the month the Company were moved from Havre to Montigny.	
			The call was brought down to Cadre Strength on 24th	

F.G Johnston Lieut
Comdg. 18th Div. Ammn. Column

WAR DIARY
or
INTELLIGENCE SUMMARY.
(Erase heading not required.)

Army Form C. 2118.

Place	Date	Hour	Summary of Events and Information	Remarks and references to Appendices
March.	1/3/19 to 15/3/19		**Officers.** During March the following Officers were dispatched to U.K. Lieut. Col. Hollins. Lieut. J.S. Devon. Lt. A. Glover.	
Montigny.	15/3/19 to 31.3.19		**Hospital** admitted during month. 2 Grs. 3 Drs. 1 S/S. **Animals.** The following were disposed of. 1-3-19. 18 L.D. 10 M. Sold. 2-3-19. 10 L.D. 20 R. To ABBEVILLE. 1-3-19 8 R. 13 L.D. 60 M. To 65 F.A. 8-3-19. 10 L.D. 40 M. To ABBEVILLE. 9-3-19. 1 L.D. 49 M. no do. 11-3-19. 3 R. To DIEPPE. 13-3-19. 5 L.D. To ABBEVILLE. 16-3-19. 12 L.D. 35 M. To ABBEVILLE. 15-3-19. 4 L.D. 53 M. Sold. 17-3-19. 1 R. 1 L.D. 3 M. Sold. 18-3-19. 6 R. To DIEPPE. 18-3-19. 1 R. 1 L.D. To M.V.S. 22-3-19. 83 Mules To 2nd Army COLOGNE. 24-3-19. 6 L.D. To DIEPPE. 24-3-19. 6 M. To 150 Co. A.S.C. 25-3-19. 2 M. To 5th F.A. 24-3-19. 1 L.D. To M.V.S.	

www.ingramcontent.com/pod-product-compliance
Lightning Source LLC
Chambersburg PA
CBHW081400160426
43193CB00013B/2076